W9-AYM-384

BERLIN

Contents

Written by Gisela Buddée
Copy edited by Katrin Wampula
Picture research by Gabriele Forst
Page layout by Cyclus · Visuelle Kommunikation

Translated by G and W Publishing and Julie Trappett
English text copy edited by Lodestone Publishing Ltd

© Falk Verlag, Ostfildern, 1. Auflage 2004
Maps © Mairs Geographischer Verlag/Falk Verlag, Ostfildern

Concept and design © Automobile Association Developments Limited
This Spiral guidebook was produced with Falk Verlag in agreement with
Automobile Association Developments Limited, owner of the "Spiral guide"
series

Published in the United States by AAA Publishing,
1000 AAA Drive, Heathrow, Florida 32746
Published in the United Kingdom by AA Publishing

ISBN 1-56251-246-3

Cover design and binding style by permission of AA Publishing

Color separation by Leo Reprographics
Printed and bound in China
by Leo Paper Products

10 9 8 7 6 5 4 3 2 1

A01737

the magazine

"Ich bin ein Berliner"

On 26 June, 1963, standing in front of Schöneberg Town Hall, US President John F Kennedy said: "*Ich bin ein Berliner*" (I am a Berliner). Approximately 3.4 million people living in Berlin can claim that – and so can a few hundred others.

But Berliners do not bear grudges; they buried her in her home town and named a square after her. Just go to the film museum in Potsdamer Platz and you'll see how much she is still considered a Berliner. Once a Berliner, always a Berliner.

Berliner by choice: John F Kennedy

Forced to be Berliners: Members of the Federal Parliame

What does it mean, to be a Berliner? In some cities you have to be born there to count as a native. In other cities it takes three or four generations before you can say you belong. But with Berlin, anyone who arrives and remains here is a Berliner.

It's Where you Live...

Take Karl Friedrich Schinkel (► 60), who was influential in shaping the city. He was born in Neuruppin in Brandenburg, but he is considered to be a Berliner – he is buried in Berlin, and the city's cemeteries are the final arbiters of who belongs here. Or take Berliner Hildegard Knef, the famous singer and actress: all right, she was born in Ulm, but Berlin sang her praises. Or Marlene Dietrich, baptised with water from the Spree river: she went to America and almost lost her Berliner citizenship as a result.

Unwilling Berliners

On 20 June, 1991, the federal parliament decided by a small majority (337 votes to 320) that, in order to complete the unity of Germany, both it and the federal government should move from the cosy ambience of Bonn to Berlin, the federal capital. To help the deputies come to terms with the move, they were offered free travel home. Housing was built for them in a remote location by the Spree, so that they could govern practically "Berlin-free". Now, however, the planes and trains back to Bonn are almost empty, and the deputies have moved into districts like Berlin-Mitte and Prenzlauer Berg, Pankow and Charlottenburg, Wedding and Friedrichshain. They have become Berliners.

Homesickness for Kurfürstendamm

It was the same for the deputies as it is for everyone else, whether from Russia or Poland, Turkey or Saxony, France, Spain or Swabia: at first the city feels almost too big and new. Then it feels small as you get to know your home patch. Soon, you find you have become a Berliner almost without noticing. Berliners who are not in Berlin are homesick. In spring 2003 a young man highjacked a plane from Istanbul to Berlin; he just wanted to come home.

Life, ah'm waitin' fer yer

Historically, Berliners have always had a relatively bad reputation. Their rulers kept out of their way, usually by moving to Potsdam. A typical Berliner is reputed to be brash and lacking in taste, but that could be interpreted as being quick-witted and

independent. In the 19th century the image of the typical Berliner came to be the layabout Nante, a figure from popular theatre. He is both cheeky and intrepid, likeable and coarse. He stands around on his street corner, ready for whatever fate brings, so long as it does not involve work. His sentiment is "Life, ah'm waitin' fer yer!"

Urban Myth or Reality?

Did President Kennedy make a German language gaffe in his historic phrase? It has been suggested that he claimed to be "a doughnut" (a *Berliner* is a particular kind of doughnut made in Berlin) and he should have said "*Ich bin Berliner*" (without the *ein*). But this is generally considered to be an urban myth and, in fact, the president's German was grammatically correct.

Page 5: Berliners and visitors at the number one attraction: the dome of the parliament building

Karl Friedrich Schinkel, master-builder of Berlin, whose style still influences Berlin today

Highlights
at a Glance

Exciting museums, imposing buildings, elegant shops and great events – these are only part of what the city has to offer. Here are some suggestions of ways to experience a true taste of Berlin.

Bus Route 100

This is more than just a bus route; it is a city tour, popular with Berliners and visitors alike. As the first east–west route since the fall of the Berlin Wall, the 100 runs from the West End (Zoologischer Garten station, past Schloss Bellevue (Bellevue Palace), the Reichstag and Unter den Linden) to the East End, passing sites of architectural, political and historical interest. The route is served each day by 24 to 30 double-deckers making a total of around 500 trips, departing every few minutes. But beware – pickpockets are always aboard! Bus 200, running from Potsdamer Platz to Prenzlauer Berg, is equally popular.

Boat Trips

Take a boat trip to experience the city from a different perspective. If you have only an hour to spare, start the "bridges tour" somewhere in Berlin-Mitte. If you have three hours and want a relaxing cruise, choose a round trip on

Especially attractive from the water: the Nikolai district

the Spree and the Landwehr canal. You'll pass by Museumsinsel (► 78–81), the new federal government buildings, industrial wharves and Charlottenburg. You'll see Potsdamer Platz from an unusual angle, then you'll be immersed in the private life of the residents of Kreuzberg on the Landwehr canal. But mind your head as you go under the bridges!

Museums as Theatre

Dance performances in the Pergamon Museum, puppet shows in front of ancient statuary, readings with music next to Nefertiti – each January and September you can see the museums in a new light. During these two months the *Lange Nacht der Museen* (Long Night of the Museums) takes place, when shuttle buses run from one museum to the next until long past midnight. You can experience jungle nights in the Botanischen Garten (Botanic Gardens), watch shadow plays and much more.

The Carnival of Cultures

Almost 450,000 foreign nationals from over 180 countries live in Berlin. When at Whitsun the "Carnival of Cultures" passes from Hermannplatz to Südstern and beyond, it looks as though they are all there: costumes from all parts of the globe, often unfamiliar musical styles

and rhythms, the traditional dances and fascinating rituals of the many varied groups parade past spectators for hours on end.

Summer Nights in the Open-air Arena

It doesn't matter whether you are going to a jazz or rock concert or an opera, the important thing is to take a picnic (and perhaps a blanket if the weather is not exactly

warm). In the heart of the city, in the dip in the Murellenberge, a mighty circular open-air arena seats 20,000 people. A twin awning protects the stage. Arrive early to get a good seat and picnic until the performance starts. It'll be wonderful, you can depend on it. (S-Bahn station: Pichelsberg.)

Bus 100 gives a good view of Schloss Bellevue

Asia in Europe at the *Karneval der Kulturen* (Carnival of Cultures)

You see bears everywhere in Berlin. They crouch on grey concrete paws by the motorway. A black and white panda bobs around in front of the Chinese embassy. Brightly painted bear statues decorate the central strip of Unter den Linden, and in the Nikolai district they crowd together in a plush-covered bunch. The top prize at the internationally renowned Berlinale film festival (► 101–2) is the "Golden Bear",and only here are teddy-bears given as awards – for the best gay and lesbian productions.

Bears are also the stars of the annual *Bärlinale* (Bearlinale), an exhibition of teddy-bears held every February. They are combed and brushed, sometimes even shampooed and washed! They sit upright or sprawl in deck chairs; some grunt, perhaps groaning in their thick clothes, while others must be freezing where their fur is worn thin from too many years of love and affection.

Thousands of bears arrive from all over Europe for the special one-day sale at the exhibition. Cuddly bears, made for the current generation of children, are for sale, but there is also an exhibition of rare and antique bears aimed strictly at the connoisseur and collector. Many famous Steiff bears have appeared at the show. "Blue Emil", for instance, one of a small batch of brightly coloured bears made in 1908, was purchased at a Bremen flea market in the early 1990s for only 3 Marks and later sold privately in London for a figure thought to be in excess of 100,000 euros! Collectors are always on the look-out for elusive rarities, such as the (possibly

Bear-O-Mania

Above: A parade of bears at Brandenburger Tor

Left: A cuddly souvenir

mythical) "green bear", purported to have been made as one of the 1908 batch. Given that the record price paid for a Steiff bear is over 150,000 euros, the "green bear" would be a valuable find!

Not surprisingly, bears are one of the top sellers at the Berlin tourist office, from the tiny, flag-waving bear pin to a traditional furry bear which comes complete with crown and *Berliner Bär* sash.

Wherever you go, Berlin is never "un-bearable"!

Origin Unknown

The mystery of Berlin's association with bears remains unsolved. All we know is that a bear appeared on a seal in 1280, but historians could not explain why it was there. It appeared again in the ordinance of the furriers' guild, and it shared the 1338 seal of the city with a margrave's eagle. Around 1500 the eagle dug its talons into the bear's neck.

In 1709 the bear stood upright, wearing a collar, when Friedrich I combined the settlements of Berlin, Cölln, Friedrichswerder, Dorotheen-stadt and Friedrichstadt to create a royal city, the first Greater Berlin. This time the bear had to share the coat of arms with the red eagle of Brandenburg and the black eagle of Prussia. In 1875 the bear was freed from its collar, and at the turn of the 20th century a five-storey crown was placed on its head. Its feathered colleagues abdicated in 1920, two years after the Kaiser, and the bear too had to lay down its crown. Now, at last, democracy could begin!

Real-life Relatives

The Berlin bear is still with us, with paws of stone or plush, on signposts and in advertisements, or decorating street corners. There are also Maxi, Schnute and Tilo, real bears living in the bear-pit behind the Märkischen Museum (U-Bahn stations: Märk, Museum). When it's the bears' birthdays, Berliners bring their heraldic beasts presents of carrot cake and other delicacies. All the same, the bears sometimes look rather unhappy – proof that they must be real Berliners!

Tilo enjoys a bear-cake

Left (page 10): A bear stands guard at the Moabiter Spree bridge

An Island in the "Red Sea"

At the end of World War II, the former Soviet Union and the Allies (Britain, France and the USA) agreed the division of the German Reich and Berlin into four occupation zones. But then the Soviet Union made its own plans, different from the Allies'.

After the war the western part of Berlin, which was surrounded by the Soviet zone, was under Allied control. At the six-power conference in London, the Allies decided to

YOU ARE LEAVING
THE AMERICAN SECTOR
ВЫ ВЫЕЗЖАЕТЕ ИЗ
АМЕРИКАНСКОГО СЕКТОРА
VOUS SORTEZ
DU SECTEUR AMÉRICAIN
SIE VERLASSEN DEN AMERIKANISCHEN SEKTOR

re-construct their zones, but the Soviets withdrew co-operation in March 1948. On 24 June, 1948, the Soviet military authorities blocked all land access to West Berlin.

The Berlin Airlift
With the mayor of Berlin Ernst Reuter, the American military governor Lucius D Clay organised an airlift. For 11 months around 2.5 million people in West Berlin were supplied by air with all the necessities of life. From coal to toilet paper and clothes to Father Christmases, there was nothing which the Allies didn't bring in to Tempelhof airport. You can see one of the planes, nicknamed *Rosinenbomber* (raisin bombers) by the people of Berlin, at the Deutsches Technikmuseum (▶ 109) near Potsdamer Platz. At the gates of Tempelhof airport a memorial commemorates this fantastic episode – Berliners call it the *Hungerharke* (hunger rake).

Shop Window of the West
In 1950 financial aid brought this "front-line city", as West Berlin was called, billions in subsidies and tax concessions. The money was spent on renewed splendour, on new districts, department stores, dance halls and film festivals which were intended to demonstrate West Berlin's will to survive as a self-governing entity. Meanwhile, firms, banks, trade associations and politicians moved away into West Germany. Despite this, West Berlin celebrated its economic miracle as the shop-window of the West.

East is East...
In 1952 the GDR leaders in the East severed all telephone lines between the eastern and

Background: A "raisin bomber"

Left: The sector boundary after the building of the Wall

Right (on page 13) from top downwards: proclamation in front of the war-damaged Reichstag; young people welcome an American "raisin bomber"; East greets West through the barbed wire; the last escape route during the building of the Wall, at Bernauer Strasse

western parts of the city. In 1953 the bus and tram links between East and West were shut down. Berliners had to walk, using the still-open sector border crossings, or take the U-Bahn or S-Bahn. Through their "voluntary construction work" the East Berliners created sports stadiums for the World Youth Festival, and the Friedrichsfelde zoo, and restored the war-damaged monuments on Unter den Linden (➤ 48) and at the Rotes Rathaus (➤ 84) and the Volksbühne (➤ 45).

Life in Isolation

On 17 June, 1953, the East Berlin workers staged an uprising against the raising of production norms. According to official figures 21 people died and 187 were injured. This day was declared a holiday by the West and named the *Tag der deutschen Einheit* (day of German unity). By 1961, 2.7 million people had fled from the East to the enticements of the "golden West". This mass exodus was endangering the work of re-construction in the East. On 13 August, 1961, the Soviet zone borders were closed, then the Wall was built. West Berlin had become an island in the "red sea".

Culture for All

A newspaper page with tips on the day's events gives you only a selection of what is on offer in Berlin – some 3,000 cultural events every day. But the real wealth of the city is that it is itself a stage.

Lights flash at night in the colonnades of the Alte Nationalgalerie, and from afar you may see shadowy figures which seem to move like ghosts. As you get nearer, you see that they are people dancing the tango to the rhythm of music from a cassette player on the ground. Anyone who wants to can join in.

A group may invite all and sundry to take their lunch break in the former GDR state bank. For an hour you can listen to classical literature. Then the readers and audience leave and go back to work.

Wings for the Imagination

A ruined department store in Oranienburger Strasse became the Tacheles art centre when the space it offered was taken over by groups of various nationalities – for sculpture, painting, showing films, invention and celebration. Some visitors did not dare to cross the threshold, what they saw seemed so strange and outside their experience. Others

Colourful graffiti art on the Tacheles building

Architecture for art – the Alte National-galerie

The Neukölln Opera

This experimental fringe opera company, with its entertaining performances and soap operas, has been a talking-point for some years. Its competition for young opera composers is unique in Germany; the winners get to see their works premiered. (Karl-Marx-Strasse 131–133, tel: (030) 68 89 07 77, U-Bahn station: Karl-Marx-Strasse)

were inspired, sought out space behind wooden partitions and in cleared-out cavities for their creativity, for music and dance, video art and fashionwear. Depopulated streets like Auguststrasse and Linienstrasse were transformed into rows of galleries. And as the imagination feeds on the incomplete, arts of every sort pop up continually in new places and disappear from the old ones, like will-o'-the-wisps. For a while places which have become well known are snapped up by location scouts for overblown commercial events. Then the champagne glasses chink in the unused U-Bahn tunnel, which yesterday saw the premiere of an opera. When it's over the builders move in.

High and Fringe Culture

There are three major opera houses and perhaps 500 other theatres whose names not even many Berliners know. Perhaps 500 theatres? Most are fringe theatres with unusual names like Tramps, Stükke, The Theatre in the Roof, Broken Windows, The Western City Stag… There are around nine cabarets, but these are now being upstaged

by comedy events. There are also puppet theatres, classical comedy houses and revue theatres. But few Berliners, when they enthuse about Berlin's culture, mean only so-called high culture or the city's 150 museums.

A Carnival of Cultures

The city itself is a theatre. It is made up of the multifarious scenes, which exist side by side, and sometimes intermingle. Chinese, Russians, Poles, Americans and Africans

The *Joker* revue at the Friedrich-stadtpalast

Fashions "Made in Berlin"

The Battle of the Cockroaches

With a shot from his revolver Nikolai Makarow, the Russian painter, begins the race and the cockroaches start running. The spectators, almost all of whom have laid bets, urge on their animals. Has Ivan the Terrible won? Crowds of people turn up at the cockroach races. There's no set fixture list, and the races are run at various venues. You can enquire at the Kaffee (Café) Burger.

Many Actors, Few Stars

Every day there are countless opportunities to ruin your evening and just a few chances to see something new and superb. Every day hundreds of aspiring actors compete in bars, halls, galleries, clubs, parks and cellars for the attention of the public. They may get very good or very bad reviews, then decide whether to continue or give up. Not many will shine even for a while in the Berlin cultural heavens. To make up for it, they put on Russian discos as in the Kaffee Burger (► 92), race cockroaches or give readings from telephone directories.

Home-grown Talent

It is probably because of nostalgia for cultural heydays like the much-lauded golden 1920s that reading fever has broken out not only in

pursue their own cultural life in Berlin, without being absorbed. A sample of these cultures goes on show every year at the Whitsun Carnival of Cultures in Kreuzberg, where samba dancers have their place just as much as cowboys and Indians (► 9).

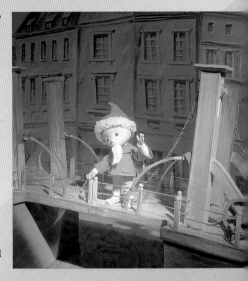

well-situated "salons" but also in trashy bars. "All my own work" has become the new high culture; be it Beatfabrik, Pyranja or Schmerzgrenze, it's all "Hiphop made in Berlin". The brand labels are all part of it, just like the attempts of young poets to capture the essence of the city in their writings.

Berlin culture means taking part, being there, even if only as an extra. Thousands of hopefuls turned up for casting as extras at Babelsberg film studios for the shooting of a new version of Jules Verne's *Around the World in Eighty Days*. They wanted to see themselves in the film standing in Gendarmenmarkt, not in Hollywood.

A film star from Babelsberg – the sandman with a GDR past

Dr Motte

In July 1989 a group of "dream-dancers" drove down Kurfürstendamm in a lorry blasting out music. Matthias Roeingh from Spandau was celebrating his 29th birthday with a demonstration with the title "Peace, Joy, Pancakes". It was the first Love Parade. The meaningless title was explained by the DJ, who had organised the first Acid House Party in Berlin, as follows: Peace stands for world peace and disarmament, Joy for international understanding through music, and Pancakes for a just distribution of food. As Dr Motte – which was his name as percussionist in the punk band Die toten Piloten (The Dead Pilots) – the inventor of the music-demo, he became a cult figure and the living mascot of the event which draws millions of ravers to Berlin on every second weekend in July. By the time the discussion about sponsors and the damage to the Tiergarten had become louder than the music, the "medium for divine love", as he saw himself, had long since abdicated and turned to designing screen-savers in a loft in Kreuzberg. But Dr Motte remains a byword in Berlin, and the party goes on.

The history of every city is reflected in its architecture. It represents the spirit of its times – in Berlin sometimes doubly so, because the Cold War was also fought with trowels and mortar.

Until World War II there was only one Berlin, whose centre was typically classical – the ruling Hohenzollern dynasty saw to that. In the city of the *Gründerzeit* (the foundation of the modern German state in 1871), and especially on Kurfürstendamm, the ornamentation drew on a mixture of neo-baroque and neo-classicism, and even at that time it was mocked as "Parvenupolis". Expressionism left few traces in Berlin's monuments, though Libeskind's Jüdisches Museum (Jewish Museum, ► 143–4) has revived it.

Fortunately, the monumental state architecture of the National Socialists got no further in its most significant plans than paper and models. Much was destroyed in the war but the monstrosities are clearly visible in what remains. The Reich Air Ministry in Leipziger Strasse, built in 1935–6 and now the Finance Ministry, is a gigantic complex. Five to seven storeys high, it is built around three closed and five open courtyards, one of which was built for ceremonial purposes. The addition of more light, greenery and technology has done little to relieve its ponderous bulk.

War of the Architects

The Cold War after the partitioning of Berlin was not limited to politics; it was also carried out on drawing-boards and in the townscape. In 1950 the East set up the "Competition for Berlin the Capital City". In the biggest urban development project of the GDR, the Stalinallee (now Karl-Marx-Allee),

"People's Palaces" were created to house workers and their families. The style: Soviet neo-classicism, combined playfully with elements drawn from Schinkel (▶ 60). In 1951 the high-rise block on Weberwiese (U-Bahn station: Weberwiese) with its pale Meissen ceramic façades formed the foundation for the whole programme. Begun in 1952, massive housing blocks in wedding-cake style rose out of the rubble on both sides of a 90-m (100-yard) wide traffic artery, 100m to 300m (100 to 300 yards) long, seven to nine storeys high, and clad with tiles. For a low rent – and countless hours of work – you got a roof terrace, refuse chute and internal telephone.

Murder and Anarchy

The West regarded this "leadership of the working classes" as an "assassination attempt on the townscape" and reacted in 1956–7 with "Interbau". International architects were to commissioned to erect, on the edges of Tiergarten, visible evidence of the "forward-looking city". Leading lights of the established modern style like Walter Gropius and Alvar Aalto, Egon Eiermann and Bruno Taut drew up plans for the Hansaviertel (Hansa quarter). For the East, however, the single blocks in the green city landscape were simply a proof of "anarchy" and "the politics of divisiveness".

Schinkel
Soviet-style:
People's
Palaces

The Workers' Revolt

It started in Block Nord, near Weberwiese U-Bahn station. On the eve of 17 June, 1953, the first workers went on strike in protest at the raising of production norms by 10 per cent. The next day workers from other factories came out in sympathy, as did some of the general population. The Soviet authorities declared a state of emergency in the city and brought in tanks, which put an end to the uprising.

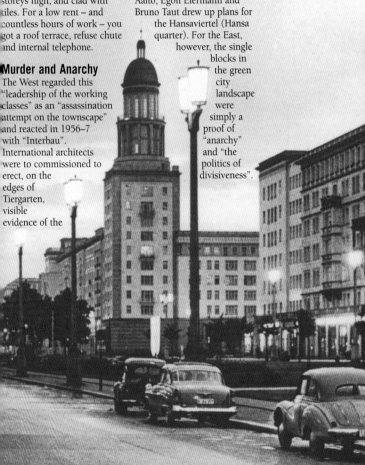

Keep Building!

Between 1961 and 1966 the Springer publishing firm built its skyscraper on Kochstrasse in Kreuzberg, 19 storeys of it, with "a view across to the other side" (U-Bahn station: Kochstrasse). The reaction from the East came between 1972 and 1977 on Leipziger Strasse: four identical blocks, 25 storeys high, with 11-storey connecting blocks, which between them effectively obscured the publishing house. The GDR praised the "differentiated colour scheme and complex structuring" of the new buildings.

Shop-window

The Europa-Center on Tauentzien (▶ 123), the first real high-rise block in West Berlin, was built between 1963 and 1965, at a time when no one expected that covered shopping arcades would become common in all districts. The 22-storey building, clad with steel and glass, with its ice-rink, restaurants and almost 100 shops, became the very image of the new "shopping experience". Until 1991 the residence of the Senator for Culture was in the Europa-Center. The 14-m (46-foot) high Mercedes star signalled to the East the strength of capitalism. East Berlin had only the revolving "B" above its cultural icon, the Berliner Ensemble theatre.

Publishing house with "a view across to the other side"

The Same for Each

The competition between the two political systems still defines the townscape. The television tower is just as much a child of the Cold War as the Philharmonia orchestra. The partitioning of the city led to duplication – of zoos, of operas, of museums and concert halls, of observatories and theatres… Anything existing in one part had to be created in the other. Each side had to prove that it didn't need the other.

Blueprints in Droves

The empty spaces which, after the fall of the Wall, made Berlin a magnet for architects from across the world, presented politicians with great dilemmas as to how to proceed. Bold architectural designs flooded the city. So it was to the relief of many, that a Berlin architect said: "A city is not an international exhibition."

Berlin is a young city, not yet 800 years old. And not only during the Cold War has it been a divided city. You can see traces of its varied history from a bird's-eye view, such as from the television tower on Alexanderplatz.

From your vantage point, look for the eight-lane concrete ribbon across the Spree behind the red-brick Rotes Rathaus and the island, the city hall and the mighty ruin of the Franciscan monastery church. You can see just how small this town was.

Overview

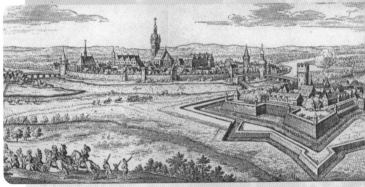

Nikolaikirche, recognisable by its twin spires. That is Mühlendamm bridge, which is where it all began. Imagine when there was just a ford here in the marshland by the Spree. Half-way between the fortresses of Spandau and Köpenick, merchants founded a small settlement; fishermen had already started to settle on a nearby island.

A Minute Triangle

In 1237 the fishermen's island of Cölln is mentioned for the first time as a town, while Berlin, lying on the ford, is not mentioned until 1244. At this time, Berlin occupied the area bounded by a traingle with points at

Tolerance Pays Off

The town grew rapidly. When Kurfürst (Electoral Prince) Friedrich Wilhelm took over as ruler of Brandenburg, the duchy was still suffering from the effects of the Thirty Years War (1618–48). The ruler married a Dutch princess, Louise of Orange. With her came the fertile province of Brabant, which supplied food for the expanding town of Berlin. As a result of the Reformation, religious refugees from Catholic Austria and France were welcomed with open arms in this Protestant town. By 1688, when Friedrich Wilhelm (the Great Elector) died, Berlin had grown to

In the 1640s the independent town of Spandau was a long way from Berlin; in 1920 it became part of Greater Berlin

20,000 inhabitants. New citizens came from France, Italy, Belgium, Switzerland, Poland and Bohemia. By the end of the 17th century there were 30,000 Berliners.

The First Greater Berlin

The Great Elector's successors were just as tolerant. In 1701 his son, known to disrespectful Berliners as *der schiefe Fritz* (crooked Fritz) because of his hunchback, had himself crowned Friedrich I of Prussia in Königsberg. The castle, originally built in 1443, was reconstructed, and the arsenal and the two churches on Gendarmenmarkt were built. On 1 January, 1710, the city was given its definitive name: Berlin. The residential area stretched approximately from the present-day railway line in the north to the cathedral in the west.

Friedrich Wilhelm, the Great Elector, welcomes the Huguenots as a support for the nation and its economy

Tall Fellows

Thrifty soldier-king Friedrich I allowed himself one extravagance for his garrison in Potsdam. Few men in Brandenburg reached the height required for his bodyguard – 1.9m (6 foot 3 inches) – so he imported tall soldiers from Czarist Russia. His son Friedrich Wilhelm I did a swop with the Dutch: 12 tall West Africans in exchange for the military bases established by his grandfather.

The city castle in Berlin-Mitte in 1788 following its reconstruction

Power Politics

Berliners hated King Friedrich Wilhelm I (1713–40), the "soldier-king", because he invested only in his army and did not risk it in a single war. When Friedrich II came to the throne, Berliners looked forward to an artistic and peace-loving king, but the young ruler marched into Silesia and waged wars which made Prussia more powerful than ever. He became known as Frederick the Great. His wars decimated both finances and people, so like his predecessors he welcomed refugees to make up the losses. His nephew Friedrich Wilhelm II (1786–97) ruled over one of the prime and, with its 150,000 inhabitants, most populous European cities.

Capital of Germany

The Rotes Rathaus (Red Town Hall, named after the colour of the bricks, not the politics) was completed in 1870. Eight main railway lines connected the "Athens of the North" with the rest of the world. In 1871 King Wilhelm I had himself crowned Emperor of Germany in Versailles, far away from his homeland. Berlin, which had been the capital of the North German Confederation since 1866, became the capital of the German Empire. In the same year, the French army was defeated at Sedan, and the *Gründerjahre* (founding years of the Empire) began. Kurfürstendamm was extended on the Parisian model, the first U-Bahn lines and a sewage system were laid. Berlin had become a metropolis.

The Boom is Over

The rapid boom came to an equally rapid end. Banks and stock exchanges were in trouble, and commercial bankruptcies led to mass redundancies and unemployment. In July 1917, three years after the start of World War I, the first peace demonstration took place. On 9 November, 1918, revolution broke out; workers went on strike. The social-democrat Philipp Scheidemann declared a republic, while from the castle Karl Liebknecht proclaimed the Free Socialist Republic of Germany and the Kaiser abdicated. Street fights, political assassinations, a general strike and a revolt followed. The social-democrats won the elections for the

Overview

Time-lapse history, from left to right: Philipp Scheidemann proclaims the Republic; Hitler becomes Reichskanzler (Chancellor), and his brown-shirt mobs march through Brandenburger Tor; books are burnt on Bebelplatz; Soviet Red Army soldiers hoist the flag of victory; women sort through the rubble for whatever is left of Berlin

National Assembly. In 1920 surrounding towns, rural communities and estates were incorporated into the city. Greater Berlin now had 4 million inhabitants.

Reign of Terror

The world slid into economic crisis in 1929; there were 450,000 unemployed in Berlin in 1930. At the elections, the National Socialist (Nazi) Party won seats in parliament. On 30 January, 1933, Adolf Hitler became Chancellor; one month later the Reichstag went up in flames. A reign of terror started: anyone thought to be left-wing was arrested, the

and his companion Eva Braun committed suicide in the Führer's bunker, about where Potsdamer Platz is now. Berlin looked like a lunar landscape, but 2.5 million people still lived in the

Above: Since 2001 the new Federal Chancellor's office has been

rubble. The victorious powers then divided the city into four sectors

communist party was banned, Jewish citizens were persecuted, books burnt, and the deportations to the extermination camps began. In September 1939, German troops invaded Poland and World War II began.

Four Sectors

In April 1945 the Soviet Red Army entered Berlin. Hitler

Capital Once More

When, in 1949, the German Democratic Republic was founded, Berlin became its capital. Forty years later, on 9 November, 1989, the border crossing on Bornholmer Strasse was reopened and Berlin became the capital and seat of government of the whole of Germany once more.

adorned by 90 tonnes of *Unity*, a sculpture by the Basque sculptor Eduardo Chillida

Berlin occupies an area of 892sq km (344 square miles). The distance from its furthest points west to east is 45km (28 miles) and from north to south it's 38km (23 miles). Berliners don't really need all that space; their *Kiez* (home patch) is good enough for them.

East or West? No one asks that question now, when you say you come from Berlin, or at any rate, not directly. But among themselves, Berliners really like to know whether someone lives in Tempelhof in the southeast or Pankow in the northeast.

And if you are

theatres, or the distance to the nearest park, swimming-pool or station. The crucial question is: if

Comfort Zones

Elegant living in Prenzlauer Berg

Bourgeois life in Charlottenburg

moving to Berlin or moving house in Berlin, then the choice of district is really important, because it will determine your quality of life.

Quality of life doesn't mean the number and type of shopping and entertainment opportunities, cinemas or

I live here, shall I still get to meet the people I know elsewhere in Berlin? The likelihood of Spandauers (from the far west of the city) flying to Bangkok is greater than their driving to Mahlsdorf (in the far east).

What would they want to go there for? Haven't they got everything they need – or even more – on their doorstep in a district of 300,000 inhabitants?

Berliners are at home in their *Kiez*. Originally a Slavonic term referring to servants' housing, *Kiez* in Berlin is synonymous with "home". In your *Kiez* you've got everything you need: baker, church, kindergarten, a friendly greeting, a cheery couple of words, a short conversation at the crossroads, a favourite bar.

Alternative living in Kreuzberg

Farewell for Ever?

Anyone moving from Kreuzberg in the south to Charlottenburg in the west may be cutting themselves off for the rest of their lives from their friends and acquaintances. You no longer run into people by chance or arrange to meet down at the corner. Sometimes you never see each other again.

Berliners move house incredibly often. They usually stay in their home patch, although they sometimes land up in a district that they don't like. At the start of the 1990s, after the fall of the Wall, many Kreuzbergers moved to Prenzlauer Berg (formerly in the East) because it reminded them of their early days in Kreuzberg, when they were young and wild and the future was uncertain. Now they are moving back to Kreuzberg. They didn't want the relaxed, chic, new-bourgeois life which had developed in Prenzlauer Berg meanwhile.

Creating your *Kiez*

The people moving in and out set the tone of a district at any given time, and soon they make it their own. Take Friedrichshain, for example: many of the dissatisfied inhabitants of this run-down working-class (blue-collar) area moved out. Young people, for whom Berlin-Mitte was too expensive, Kreuzberg too traditional and Prenzlauer Berg too manicured and intellectual, moved into the cheap housing in Friedrichshain. They opened lively shops and bars and created their own *Kiez*, quite different from its former character.

Berliners don't see the point of green spaces unless they can lie around, barbecue or play games on them. Prohibitions irritate them.

The "Cosmos" spare-time footballers are warming up. Since 1993 they have played on the lawns in front of the Reichstag building. Now there's a notice with a flower on it, saying *Geschützte Grünanlage* (Protected Grass Area). And just so that everyone gets the point, there's also a red circle with a crossed-out footballer in it. The authorities are threatening footballers with a red card. Persistent offenders

Above: Sunday picnic in the Tiergarten

Left: Grunewaldsee – a dog's paradise

Summer in the City

are to be fined 50 euros. The lawn is now designated a "sunbathing lawn". But it's not yet certain who's going to win this battle. Berliners don't give up their "acquired rights" as easily as that.

Picnic in the Tiergarten

Anyone going down to the little Schloss Bellevue (Bellevue Palace) in the Tiergarten will be greeted by the smell of barbecuing. Extended Turkish families will have set out early with rugs, garden chairs, tables, crockery, barbecues, charcoal and food. They'll spend the day in the Tiergarten, eating and drinking, playing games, dreaming skywards and making themselves thoroughly at home. When

Right: There's always space for roller-blading

drive out on a Sunday to the Grunewaldsee. It has become a local saying: "It's pointless to be dogless in the Grunewald" because you would just feel lonely and aimless. Dozens of dogs of all sizes cluster around the fast-food stalls (stands), swim after balls at Hundestrand (Dogs' Beach) – which actually exists – and carry sticks around.

There's Something for Everyone in a Park

The kick-boxers' Eldorado lies in the gardens behind Schloss Charlottenburg while, to the north of Charlottenburg, Volkspark Jungfernheide attracts swimmers, hikers and boating enthusiasts; there are also sports fields.

In the mornings the plastic swords used in oriental exercises clatter against each other in, among others, Viktoriapark; many people come here just to enjoy the view from the park's summit. Lovers of evening campfires meet in Mauerpark. In Hasenheide jugglers will have been practising long before naked young men roast in the sun on the little private gays' meadow there. Cross this park on a warm summer evening and Brazilian drums will accompany you. But be aware that, as with many urban parks, it is advisable not to stay after dark, however much you may like the music.

The most important activity on Berlin summer days is to go to a park. It doesn't really matter which park, each one is different and is used for all sorts of things, especially ball games and jogging. Berliners don't worry about the notices that say *Ballspielen verboten* (No ball games allowed) – they are everywhere and are generally ignored!

they have left, the crows will empty the rubbish bins searching for anything edible.

Drama at the Lakeside

If you would like to hear actors learning their lines, then head for the Schlachtensee where you can walk with them round the lake. If you want to study the social behaviour of urban dogs, then

WATERSIDE CITY

There are 190km (120 miles) of waterway and almost 2,000 bridges in Berlin. But only recently have Berliners discovered that ships aren't the only things that can travel on water.

The boat rocks on the Havel river, the owner is reading his newspaper under a sunshade, his wife chats to her neighbour. She is standing up to her waist in water, and so is the neighbour. An hour later nothing has changed. Not all boat-owners are as resolute as that, but on warm summer days, when it is as hot in the city as in the far south, the ducks seem to be the only things moving on the water. Boat owners will have checked at the start of the fine weather period that the boat *can* move.

Life On Your Dream Boat

The writer Tucholsky wrote of his dream of a "villa in the country with a wide terrace, before you the Baltic, behind you Friedrichstrasse, great view, rural chic, from the bathroom you can see the Zugspitze… (a mountain in the Bavarian Alps)". If you take a boat trip to

A waterside site for the Ministry of the Interior

Chilling out at Kreuzberg Urbanhafen (Urban Harbour)

Charlottenburg, you'll see that quite a few people have set up their dream houseboat on the Spree. On the Plötzenseer Kolk too, by the Saatwinkel dam, you'll see washing drying on board. The owners of these houseboats must be skilled craftspeople and masters of the highest levels of diplomacy in their relations with officials and authorities

Taking the plunge into the Spree

A Berliner's dream: a houseboat on the banks of the Spree

– because officially these houseboats do not exist. At least, not yet.

By the Water not *on* the Water

The concept of a "waterside city" assumes that its inhabitants live *by* the water, not *on* it. Once the first companies and embassies had developed the best sites, housing was built right up to the river banks. Then there grew a desire for floating houses: not houseboats, but proper homes on the water. "Berlin was built from barges," they say – in the city's history the water was always a transport artery, as it still is. But is it a good place to live?

Floating Homes

As a result of an architectural competition called "Floating Homes", designs have been reviewed, but the authorities have not yet agreed on a plan of action. Meanwhile Berliners continue to rock up and down on restaurant boats in the urban harbour or by Oberbaum bridge, sit in the open-air cinema on the Insel der Jugend (Island of Youth) opposite Treptower Park and go swimming at more than 40 bathing places or at 31 open-air swimming-pools.

Of course, you could always hire a boat – everything from a canoe to a sailing boat – and explore Berlin's network of lakes and waterways for yourself.

Did You Know

... that in the Ritz Carlton Schlosshotel you can sleep in Karl Lagerfeld's bed, if you don't mind paying for it? When he was planning the rooms, the fashion designer took out a lifetime reservation on a suite for himself.

... that there are 83,000 allotment holders in Berlin? They are a powerful political force and protest vehemently against any proposal to use allotment land for other purposes. In 1987 they even threatened to found their own party.

... that the Noack foundry produces complete statues? Rainer Fettings' statue of Willy Brandt, which stands in the Kreuzberg offices of the SPD (Social Democratic Party), was made here. *The Quadriga* (four-horsed chariot) on top of Brandenburger Tor was cast here, and the workshop contains a statue of Frederick the Great, as well as works by Henry Moore, Georg Kolbe and Joseph Beuys.

... that the 2.7ha (6½-acre) Chinese Garden in Berlin-Marzahn is the largest in Europe?

... that the geographical centre of Berlin is on Alexandrinenstrasse in Kreuzberg? Exact location: 52°, 30', 10" north, 13°, 24', 15" east.

... that in 1987 a World Cup ski race was held on the Teufelsberg in the Grunewald – on grass?

... that Berlin has the Allies to thank for having no closing time? It was in fact Heinz Zellermeyer, the head of the hotels and inns guild, who in 1949 instigated its abolition. After years of curfew Berlin has now revived its pre-war bar culture.

... that on 20 April, 1830, the dog tax was introduced in Berlin? At that time there were 6,000 dogs in the city (today there are 94,000). Some city politicians wanted to forbid the poorer classes from owning dogs at all, because it was deemed they had no possessions for dogs to guard.

Finding Your Feet

First Two Hours

Tegel Airport (TXL)

Berlin has three airports. Otto Lilienthal airport at Tegel deals with international flights to Western Europe and the USA, with internal German connections. It's about 8km (5 miles) from the western and 10km (6 miles) from the eastern side of the city.

Airport Transfers

- Depending on the time of day and the traffic, a **taxi** into the city will take 15 to 30 minutes and cost about 20 euros.
- **JetExpressbus** TXL connects Alexanderplatz and Unter den Linden with the airport, takes 20 to 30 minutes and costs 2–3 euros.
- **Expressbus X9** goes to Zoologischer Garten station and costs 2–3 euros.
- **Bus 109** takes you to Jakob-Kaiser-Platz, where you change onto U-Bahn train U7. The journey costs 2–3 euros.
- Buses depart about every 10 minutes during the week; at weekends every 20 minutes.

Schönefeld Airport (SXF)

This airport lies about 20km (12-miles) to the southeast of the city centre. It deals with flights from eastern and southeastern Europe, from the Near East and from Asia, as well as with charter flights.

Airport Transfers

- Depending on the time of day, a **taxi** into the city will take about 30 minutes and cost about 30 euros.
- The **Airport-Express** trains (Regionalbahn RE4 and RE55) depart hourly via Ostbahnhof, Alexanderplatz and Friedrichstrasse to Zoologischer Garten station.
- The **S9** (via Ostbahnhof and Hackescher Markt to Spandau) and the **S45** (Neukölln, Schöneberg and Wedding) also link the city centre with the airport.

Tempelhof Airport (THF)

This inner-city airport is used mainly for regional traffic. Take the U-Bahn from Platz der Luftbrücke station. The airport may be closed permanently soon, but no date has yet been set.

Central Flight Information

Tel: 0180/500 01 86

Railway Stations

Trains stop at Zoologischer Garten station (Hardenbergplatz 11) and at Ostbahnhof (Strasse der Pariser Kommune 5). Motorail trains all come in to Wannsee station (Kronprinzessinnenweg).

- Information on **train times** and **ticket prices**: tel: 01805/99 66 33; www.bahn.de

Buses

National and international long-distance coaches arrive at the Zentraler Omnisbusbahnhof (Central Bus Station) in the Internationales Congress Centrum (ICC, Masurenallee 4–6).

- **Information**: tel: (030) 302 53 61; **reservations**: tel: (030) 30 10 38 20.

Cars

All main roads and motorways join the **Berliner Ring** (the A10), from which you branch off to your destination.

Tourist Information

Comprehensive information can be obtained from Berlin Tourismus Marketing GmbH, Am Karlsbad 11, D-10785 Berlin; fax: (030) 25 00 24 24; www.btm.de

- There are tourist information centres at: the **Europa-Center**, entrance at Budapester Strasse 45, Mon–Sat 10–7, Sun 10–6; **Brandenburger Tor**, south wing, daily 10–6; **Info Café** below the television tower, Alexanderplatz, daily 10–6. Apr–Oct opening times are longer.
- **Reservations**: (030) 25 00 25; from outside Germany tel: 49 700 86 23 75 46.

Getting Around

Berlin has an excellent U-Bahn (underground/subway) and S-Bahn (local commuter) railway system, complemented by bus and trams routes; it also has a good cycle network. From spring to autumn, cycle taxis ferry people around, mainly through the parks. Most boats are pleasure cruisers, but in Köpenick there are also ferry services.

Public Transport

- In 2002 the Berlin U-Bahn system celebrated its centenary. Around 400 million passengers are transported annually on about 144km (almost 90 miles) of track. There are 170 stations, of which 79 are buildings of historical and architectural interest.
- Nine **U-Bahn lines** run from 4 am to 2 am the next day. On Saturday, Sunday and public holidays a 24-hour service operates. Sections which are not serviced by the U-Bahn are covered by night buses.
- Fifteen **S-Bahn lines** generally operate round the clock. A circle line is again running around the city centre, as it did before World War II.
- Almost all the **tram routes** are in the east of the city. The only new stretch is in Wedding (in the west).
- There are three **price zones**: A for the area inside the S-Bahn circle line, B as far as the city boundaries, and C for the surrounding country. With an AB ticket you can travel around the whole of Berlin.

Tickets

- Single tickets are valid for two hours. With a **Kurzstreckenkarte** (short journcy tickct) you can travel three stations on the S-Bahn and up to six on a bus or the U-Bahn.
- You can buy tickets at railway stations, but also at kiosks, in tobacconists and anywhere you see the sign **"BVG-Karten"**.
- **Children** under 6 and dogs travel free. For children aged 7 to 14 there is a reduced tariff.
- For **cycles** you pay the normal fare.
- You can buy **travel cards** valid for one to seven days.
- For tourists there is the **WelcomeCard**, giving three days' free travel and various reductions at attractions in Berlin and Potsdam.
- You must **validate** your ticket for each journey. There are validating machines on U-Bahn and S-Bahn platforms and in buses.
- The **penalty for travelling without a valid ticket** is 60 euros.

City Tours

There are many companies offering city tours. The tours start on **Kurfürstendamm** (corner of Fasanenstrasse, opposite Breitscheidplatz and the Europa-Center) or on **Unter den Linden** (Pariser Platz and corner of Friedrichstrasse), and they last between 1 and 3 hours. The tours give live commentaries, sometimes in two languages. On some tours you can listen to commentaries on headphones in one of six languages, though the taped information may be out of date.

Cycling

■ The railway system has 1,700 **"Callbikes"** waiting to be used, mainly at crossroads. You hire and return the bikes by phone (the number is on the bike). You pay by credit or debit card.

■ You can also **hire bikes** at: Hackesche Höfe in Berlin-Mitte, tel: (030) 28 38 48 48; Auguststrasse 29, tel: (030) 28 59 96 61; Friedrichstrasse 141, tel: (030) 20 45 45 00; and Bergmannstrasse 9 in Kreuzberg, tel: (030) 215 15 66.

Taxis

There are taxi ranks at airports, railway stations, shopping centres, organised events and the larger squares. You can hail a taxi if its sign is illuminated. The big Berlin taxi firms share a single free number: 0800/800 11 44, which connects you to whichever firm is not busy.

Velotaxi (Cycle Taxi)

High-tech tricycles have been transporting passengers since 1997, using bus lanes, cycle tracks and parks. You just hail them if they are empty. There are ranks at Wittenbergplatz, Adenauerplatz, Zoo, Brandenburger Tor and Alexanderplatz.

Cars

Traffic is less dense in Berlin than in most other big cities, but parking is just as much a problem. In the city centre there is no free parking. Half an hour's parking will cost you 1 euro. In many areas you can park free in the evening and on Saturday and Sunday afternoon, though around the Hackesche Höfe you have to pay at any time.

On Foot in Berlin

A host of organisations offer walking tours on various themes, through the historic old town, to ministries or embassies, to famous cemeteries, hill walks, through individual districts or "green Berlin" or in the steps of writers and poets. The commentaries are in German, sometimes in English, French or Italian. You will find information brochures in the tourist information centres (► 35) or on the tourist information website: www.berlin-tourist-information.de.

By Plane

If you would like to experience Berlin from the air, from a *Rosinenbomber* (► 12), helicopter or seaplane, then contact Air Service Berlin, tel: (030) 53 21 53 21; www.commanderfrank.de

By Boat

Almost 200km (125 miles) of waterways are used by shipping companies of all sizes for tours and excursions. The tours on offer range from trips through historic Berlin to round trips through the city and the seven lakes, excursions to Köpenick or Potsdam or canal locks in Brandenburg, to nocturnal outings. The three biggest firms are Stern und Kreis Schifffahrt (sales office in Treptow harbour, tel: 030 536 36 00, www.SternundKreis.de), Reederei Riedel (tel: 030 691 37 82, www.reederei-riedel.de) and Reederei Bruno Winkler (tel: 030 349 95 95, www.reedereiwinkler.de). Information brochures are available from the tourist information centres (➤ 35).

Berlin Place Names

For a guide to the German language and Berlin place names, see Useful Words and Phrases (➤ 189–90).

Admission Charges
The cost of admission to museums and places of interest mentioned in this guide is indicated by three price categories:
inexpensive under 3 euros
moderate 3–6 euros
expensive over 6 euros

The *SchauLust-Museen Berlin* three-day museum pass gives entry to more than 50 museums. You can buy it at the museums or in the tourist information centres (➤ 35).

Accommodation

You have the choice of over 60,000 beds in more than 500 hotels and the supply is still increasing, especially in luxury class hotels and in inexpensive hostels for backpackers. The selection of accommodation on pages 38–41 includes designer hotels and hotels catering only for women, and for visitors with children.

City Districts

Almost all hotels in Berlin-Mitte have been opened, or at least modernised, in the last ten years. Those in Prenzlauer Berg are all new. Nearly all the back-packer hostels are also found in these two districts or in Kreuzberg. Some of the hotels around the Kurfürstendamm continue to uphold the traditions of the past with their spacious, somewhat grandiose suites frequented, not only during film festivals, by celebrities. The accommodation on offer also includes guest houses characterised by their solicitous landladies, plush sofas and inherited artworks. Berlin is proud of its great gay and lesbian scene and publicises it widely, both within Germany and abroad. In the official city accommodation lists, hotels indicate by means of a rainbow ribbon that they are gay and lesbian friendly. Most of these hotels are in the western and eastern city centre.

Reservations

You can book into any partner hotel of Berlin Tourismus Marketing GmbH by phone on (030) 25 00 25, by fax on (030) 25 00 24 24, or online at www.berlin-tourist-information.de. You can obtain a list of these partner hotels from Am Karlsbad 11, 10785 Berlin. Any other hotel can usually be booked on the internet.

Private Accommodation

Rooms and apartments can be rented privately. You can find out about them at tourist information centres (➤ 35) or from the letting agency at Mehringdamm 66, 10961 Berlin, tel: (030) 786 20 03, fax: (030) 785 06 14, www.wohnen-berlin.de

Campsites

Berlin has six campsites. The best and biggest, with 450 spaces, is Am Krossinsee in Köpenick (Wernstorfer Strasse 45, 12579 Berlin, tel: (030) 675 86 87, fax: (030) 675 91 50); it's open all year round, has a separate youth area, a pub and holiday chalets, and you can hire bikes and boats. Or try Deutscher Camping Club Berlin, Geisbergstrasse 11, tel: (030) 218 60 71.

Hotels

> **Accommodation Prices**
> Prices for a double room with breakfast:
> € under 70 euros
> €€ 70–120 euros
> €€€ 120–180 euros
> €€€€ over 180 euros
>
> Hotel prices in Berlin are relatively moderate. Apart from during big events (Love Parade, trade fairs), you will also have a good chance of negotiating special rates.

acksel Haus Berlin €–€€

This beautiful little private hotel is in an excellent position in Prenzlberg, only a few minutes walk from the Wasserturm with its numerous cafés and restaurants and from Kollwitzplatz. The rooms are mostly individually styled apartments: in the Africa room you sleep in a sand-coloured tent; you share the "Movie" room with photos of stars of the screen; and the elegant styling of the "Venice" room really shows off the mouldings to their best advantage. In summer you can relax on a divan amidst the greenery of the pretty inner courtyard.

➕ 193 F4 ✉ Belforter Strasse 21
☎ (030) 44 33 76 33; fax (030) 441 61 16; www.ackselhaus.de
🚇 Senefelder Platz

Adlon Kempinski €€€€

Albert Einstein, Charlie Chaplin and Thomas Mann stayed in the legendary old Adlon. The star visitor of the new Adlon is Michael Jackson. The opulence of a golden age survives here unaltered, liveried butlers carry your luggage, the rooms and suites glisten with gilded finery and the latest in luxury. The presidential suite has a fine view over Brandenburger Tor (Brandenburg Gate) and Unter den Linden.

➕ 192 B2 ✉ Unter den Linden 77
☎ (030) 226 10; fax (030) 22 61 22 22; www.hotel-adlon.de
🚇 Unter den Linden

Alexander Plaza €€€

From this inviting hotel, situated in the centre of Berlin-Mitte, it is only a few steps to Alexanderplatz, Unter den Linden, the synagogue in Oranienburger Strasse or the Hackescher Markt. Some of the light, spacious rooms have the added bonus of a view directly onto the Hackesche Höfe. Meals are served in the pretty Winter Garden restaurant. After sight-seeing you can relax in the hotel's sauna or prepare for the evening in the fitness room.

⊞ 193 D3 ⊠ Rosenstrasse 1
☎ (030) 24 00 10; fax (030) 24 00 17 77; www.hotel-alexander-plaza.de
Ⓖ Hackescher Markt

Bleibtreu €€€–€€€€

This pleasant, central hotel has a beautiful lobby with a scent evocative of flowers and delicatessen counters, and a romantic courtyard. Situated in a side street off the Kurfürstendamm, it has been equipped with an eye to your health. Under the one roof you can sleep, eat, relax and shop: in the Turkish bath (included in the price) you can forget the stresses of sight-seeing, attended by a health therapist. And if you don't make it to breakfast in the restaurant or espresso bar, you can have it sent up using the TV display in your room.

⊞ 194 A3 ⊠ Bleibtreustrasse 31
☎ (030) 88 47 40; fax (030) 88 47 44 44; www.bleibtreu.com
Ⓖ Uhlandstrasse

Boarding House Mitte €€–€€€

Coffee, tea and pastries greet you on arrival here. The generously furnished apartments in an excellent position, just by Hackescher Markt, are a genuine alternative to a hotel for anyone who wants to feel at home in Berlin. You can have rolls delivered to complement your own breakfast, a shopping service saves you the chore of lugging in carrier bags after a day's sight-seeing, and the room service even washes your dirty dishes in the apartment's kitchen. From the maisonnette apartment on the top floor you have a marvellous view over the centre of Berlin.

⊞ 193 E3 ⊠ Mulackstrasse 1
☎ (030) 28 38 84 88; fax (030) 28 38 84 89; www.boardinghouse-mitte.com
Ⓖ Weinmeisterstrasse

Bogota €–€€

With its characteristic high ceilings, rooms in a variety of interesting shapes and sizes, and the furniture in its lobby and breakfast room, this hotel near Kurfürstendamm has all the charm of a plush Berlin private house from 1911. Children are welcome and stay free of charge in their parents' room.

⊞ 194 A3 ⊠ Schlüterstrasse 45
☎ (030) 881 50 01; fax (030) 883 58 87; www.HotelBogota.de
Ⓖ Adenauerplatz

Die Fabrik – Hostel Kreuzberg €

This former factory has been turned into a chic 5-storey hostel. At first glance only the existence of the communal bathrooms betrays its origin. The spacious rooms, simply but individually furnished, and the lobby have an early 20th-century charm. Breakfast and all other meals are taken in the "alternative" atmosphere of the adjoining Café Eisenwaren. The best thing about the hostel is the studio on the top floor with its sloping glass roof – and the luxury of its own wash-basin! Hot water for the whole building is provided by means of the solar panels on the roof.

⊞ 198 C2 ⊠ Schlesische Strasse 18
☎ (030) 611 71 16; fax (030) 618 29 74; www.diefabrik.com
Ⓖ Schlesisches Tor

Dorint Schweizerhof Berlin €€€€

This modern business hotel by the Zoo station looks out onto the zoo opposite or onto a shady inner courtyard. All rooms are stylish and functional, and those offered as business rooms provide plenty of working space. Nor is there any shortage of ways to relax: you can forget hectic city life in Berlin's biggest hotel pool; the Mediterranean restaurant and beer bar offer various tasty dishes, and you can have the last drink of the day in the open lobby bar. In 2003 the hotel was voted the friendliest in the business hotel category.

⊞ 194 C3 ⊠ Budapester Strasse 25
☎ (030) 269 60; fax (030) 26 96 10 00; www.dorint.com
Ⓖ Zoologischer Garten

Gates €€–€€€

Europe's first internet hotel, where stars like Claudia Cardinale and Marlon Brando used to stay, has a renovated late 19th-century façade and a listed grand staircase. Now it is fitted out with de luxe ICT facilities – PCs with flat screens and CD-ROM drives. The high-speed internet connection is free of charge and has no time limit. Rates are cheaper if you book a room online.

➕ 194 A4 ✉ Knesebeckstrasse 8–9
☎ (030) 31 10 60;
fax (030) 312 20 60;
www.hotel-gates.com
Ⓖ Ernst-Reuter-Platz

Gendarm €€€

The concert hall and the Deutscher and Französischer Dom (German and French churches, ➤ 59) are right on your doorstep and, if you're lucky, just outside your window. The 20 rooms and 10 suites of this family-run hotel are elegantly furnished. For relaxation after a strenuous day's sightseeing there is a sauna, a solarium, a fitness room and a bar.

➕ 192 C1 ✉ Charlottenstrasse 61
☎ (030) 206 06 60;
fax (030) 20 60 66 66;
www.hotel-gendarm-berlin.de
Ⓖ Stadtmitte

Grand Hyatt Berlin €€€€

The Spanish architect José Rafael Moneo and the Swiss designer Hannes Wettstein planned and furnished this luxury hotel on Potsdamer Platz. Modern art, contemporary design and top-class materials are all an important part of the concept. The Olympus Spa club on the seventh floor is superb: you can swim in a pool and look out over the city. An excellent restaurant, a bar with 200 varieties of whisky, a bistro and live jazz in the evening are all on offer.

➕ 196 A4 ✉ Marlene-Dietrich-Platz 2 ☎ (030) 25 53 12 34;
fax (030) 25 53 12 35;
www.berlin.hyatt.com
Ⓖ Potsdamer Platz

Greifswald €€

In one of the courtyards you can experience the typical Prenzlauer Berg flair, breakfasting on home-cooked fare. The tram runs past the door, Alexanderplatz is just three stops away, and Kollwitzplatz with its many restaurants and bars is a few minutes' walk away.

➕ 193, east of F4 ✉ Greifswalder Strasse 211 ☎ (030) 442 78 88;
fax: (030) 442 78 98;
www.hotel-greifswald.de
🚋 100, Tram 2, 3, 4

Hecker's Hotel €€€–€€€€

This little hotel, renowned for its friendliness, earns its reputation anew every day. The double rooms are equipped with walk-in wardrobe, kitchenette and marble bath. The themed suites are fitted out in German colonial, Bauhaus or Tuscan style. In the evening you can enjoy a glass of wine on the balcony while you watch the lively scene on Kurfürstendamm.

➕ 194 A3 ✉ Grolmannstrasse 35
☎ (030) 889 00; fax (030) 889 02 60;
www.heckers-hotel.com
Ⓖ Savignyplatz

Honigmond Garden Hotel €€–€€€

Really attractive apartments surround a green courtyard garden in this delightful hotel. Instead of the noise of traffic, you hear water splashing at breakfast and frogs croaking in the evening – and yet it's only a short walk to Friedrichstrasse, Hackescher Markt and Museumsinsel.

➕ 192 B4 ✉ Invalidenstrasse 122
☎ (030) 28 44 55 77;
fax (030) 28 44 55 88;
www.honigmond-berlin.de
Ⓖ Zinnowitzer Strasse

Intermezzo-women's hotel €

This welcoming women's hotel lies between Brandenburger Tor and Potsdamer Platz (males aged 12 or under may also check in). By bus it's only two stops to Unter den Linden. The rooms, panelled in light wood, all have a shower; toilets are mostly down the corridor. Three- and four-bedded rooms are available for women travelling together.

➕ 192 B1 ✉ Gertrud-Kolmar-Strasse 5 ☎ (030) 22 48 90 96; fax (030) 22 48 90 97; www.hotelintermezzo.de

🚇 Potsdamer Platz

Kinderinsel €

This is pure child-land; everything is bright and exciting – and the staff can speak 12 languages between them. Children can decide whether to sleep in the jungle or in a cosy room. Qualified teachers are on hand to care for children round the clock, offering a stimulating and creative programme of activities. And the in-house catering ensures a child-orientated menu – morning, noon and evening.

➕ 192 C4 ✉ Eichendorffstrasse 17 ☎ (030) 41 71 69 28; fax (030) 41 71 69 48; www.kinderinsel.de

🚇 Zinnowitzer Strasse

Künstlerheim Luise €€

Whether you want a room in the roof with shower outside or a suite with a bath, behind every door of this listed, classical, 1825 palace a different world awaits you. To put it another way, each of the 45 rooms is a work of art, designed by a different living artist. You can view them all on the internet: for example, there's Rainer Gross's simple "Shaker Life", Peter Büchler's totally white "Horse Astronaut", or perhaps you would prefer Elvira Bach's black-and-white room with its outsize female figures. A portion of the revenue from the room goes to the artist. The hotel's WeinGuy restaurant is well known.

➕ 192 B2 ✉ Luisenstrasse 19 ☎ (030) 28 44 80; fax (030) 28 44 84 48; www.kuenstlerheim-luise.de

🚇 Friedrichstrasse

Lette'm sleep €

This typical backpacker hostel is in the middle of Prenzlauer Berg with its bars, dives and clubs. The welcoming rooms, furnished in light woods, accommodate up to six people; baths and toilets are along the corridor; in the two-bed rooms there is even a small kitchenette. People get together in the bright, comfortable common room, which has cooking facilities and free internet access.

➕ 193, north of F5 ✉ Lettestrasse 7 ☎ (030) 44 73 36 23; fax (030) 44 73 36 25; www.backpackers.de

🚇 Prenzlauer Allee

Mitte's backpacker hostel €

This attractive backpacker hostel in Berlin-Mitte, has individually styled rooms. Bathrooms are along the corridor. Whether there are two of you in the honeymoon room or several in a four-person room, travellers with a limited budget will find this an inexpensive lodging and an ideal starting point for sight-seeing and night-life. You can cater for yourself in the kitchen, and there is a laundry service, internet café and bike hire.

➕ 192 B4 ✉ Chausseestrasse 102 ☎ (030) 28 39 09 65; fax (030) 28 39 09 35; www.backpacker.de

🚇 Zinnowitzer Strasse

Riehmers Hofgarten €€

Originally a *fin de siècle* apartment block built for wealthy Berliners, the Riemers Hofgarten was remodelled in 1999. The 20 good-sized rooms offer contemporary style combined with modern functionalism.

➕ 196 A1 ✉ Yorckstrasse 83 ☎ (030) 780 98 800; fax (030) 780 98 808; www.riehmers-hofgarten.de

🚇 Mehringdamm

Unter den Linden €€

A modern, former GDR, centrally located hotel on the corner of Friedrichstrasse and Unter den Linden, this hotel has 331 comfortably furnished rooms. The "Tilia" bar and restaurant has gorgeous views over Unter den Linden, and there is a summer terrace for an alfresco drink or meal.

➕ 192 B2 ✉ Unter den Linden 14 ☎ (030) 238 11 10; fax (030) 23 81 11 00; www.hotel-unter-den-linden.de

🚇 Friedrichstrasse

Food and Drink

Meatballs, *Eisbein* (knuckle of pork) with pureed peas, liver with apple-rings and onions – Berlin's traditional cuisine is hardly ever on the menu. The modern cuisine is called "Crossover" and is likely to show an Asian influence. It's taking over the traditional eateries as well.

Berlin's culture of snacking is legendary. *Currywurst* (sausage with curry sauce), "invented" in 1949 as an homage to American spare ribs with ketchup, has knocked cold meatballs and hot-dogs off the top of the popularity stakes. If you order a *currywurst* in Berlin you will be asked *"Mit oder ohne?"* which means, with or without potato skins, crispy or soft. One *currywurst* stand has even become famous, Konnopke in Prenzlauer Berg (► 165). Kreuzbergers prefer to get their *currywurst* on Mehringdamm, and night-owls look for theirs at Kurfürstendamm 196, served on china plates, perhaps with a glass of bubbly.

Most Popular Snack: Doner
With more than 1,300 stalls (stands) throughout the city the Turkish doner kebab is a long way ahead of the snack field (though filled bagels, exotic soups and oriental snacks are catching up fast): a piece of pitta bread, some minced lamb, salad, onions, cabbage and perhaps a shot of garlic sauce, and your meal is ready.

Soljanka Soup
Remarkable East–West differences can still be seen on the menus of simpler restaurants. In the former East Berlin almost all restaurant menus feature *soljanka*, a soup which often serves to use up left-overs but which in Russia is a thick soup containing pieces of sausage, gherkins and lemon, topped with sour cream. You won't find this "GDR-soup" in the former West Berlin, though – all the Hungarian, Polish and Russian eating-houses have disappeared from the townscape.

Not So Traditional
Traditional Berlin dishes like knuckle of pork or liver can be found, with a few exceptions, only in traditional restaurants like Zur letzten Instanz (► 89) and inns catering for excursions. Traditional fish recipes, using fresh fish like pike and perch from the River Havel, have been adapted, updated and brought into the new "light" cuisine.

Metropolitan Cuisine
It's typical of today's Berlin that you can eat Italian, Turkish, Greek, Spanish, French, Russian, Mexican and Brazilian, African, Australian and American, Vietnamese, and Japanese food. Increasingly, you find pan-Asiatic dishes and even bold experimental fare. Vegetarian restaurants often also serve fish dishes in addition to their standard menus.

Open-Air Eating
As soon as the sun shines, Berlin landlords set up tables on the pavement (sidewalk) or in the garden. It's great sitting outside in the city. Inexpensive menus are often offered at lunch-time, usually from noon to 3 pm. Quite a few restaurants are open all day, but most open only after 6 in the evening. There are inns on the banks of the Havel (Moorlake, Blockhaus Nikolskoe) and of the Spree (Klipper in Treptow) which specialise in catering for excursion

buses. These inns are included in excursion itineraries because they offer fine views across the rivers.

Just Breakfast

In almost all Berlin cafés you can have breakfast at any time till 4 pm, sometimes even later. Many cafés have a Sunday buffet where you pay a fixed charge and eat as much as you want.

Berliner Weisse (white beer)

And what do Berliners drink after breakfast? Usually beer. Besides the two big breweries (Schultheiss and Berliner Kindl) there are a number of small private breweries. The Huguenots first brewed *Berliner Weisse*, which has become a tradition. It's a top-fermented beer which is drunk with a straw out of wide bowls, with a "green shot" (woodruff syrup) or a "red shot" (raspberry syrup). *Weisse* is low-alcohol, so it's a refreshing summer drink.

Prices
Restaurants are described in each of the main sections of this guide, with indicative prices per person, without drinks, as follows:
€ under 12 euros
€€ 12–25 euros
€€€ over 25 euros

Shopping

Shopping is one of the main pleasures for most visitors to Berlin. Away from the traditional business streets, Kurfürstendamm and Friedrichstrasse, there are many enticing little shops selling out-of-the-ordinary items, and markets for food, handicrafts and antiques.

Souvenirs

■ Almost every visitor to Berlin takes home a souvenir. Bears of all sorts beckon (► 10–11); ashtrays featuring pictures of Brandenburger Tor are popular, as are beer tankards bearing the Berlin coat of arms. T-shirts in all sizes and a multitude of designs are sold in great quantities, and the sellers of genuine pieces of the Berlin Wall are not doing badly either. Fluffy flakes, black from exhaust fumes, fall in glass "snow scenes" on gaudy Trabants (a small car mass-produced in the GDR). You'd think that all the caps of the GDR's National People's Army must by now be scattered across the globe, but you can still buy them here, along with Soviet watches with their characteristic red star.
■ Pieces of **fine china** from the former royal factory, to be found on Kurfürstendamm or Unter den Linden, are souvenirs which will hold their value better.

Fashion and Design

Fashion accessories by designers from across the world can be bought on the "Kudamm" (Kurfürstendamm) and Friedrichstrasse. You'll find many small fashion shops and witty Berlin labels in Schlüterstrasse in Charlottenburg and in Alte and Neue Schönhauser Strasse in Berlin-Mitte. New, innovative accessories for the kitchen and bathroom are created by designers with shops in Winterfeldtplatz and Goltzstrasse in Schöneberg, in Bergmannstrasse in Kreuzberg and in Kastanienallee in Prenzlauer Berg.

Art

There are more than 100 art galleries showing works by painters, sculptors, photographers and craftspeople. Most artists show their work in the area around Auguststrasse, Oranienstrasse, Linienstrasse and Torstrasse. A new artistic quarter has grown up under the railway arches along the Spree in Holzmarktstrasse. Many galleries are located in the west of the city, north of Kurfürstendamm, between Giesebrechtstrasse and Uhlandstrasse.

Markets

Every week more than 100 markets are held in Berlin. They are mostly weekly markets of various sizes, selling fruit and vegetables. Almost every district also has its junk or flea market, usually held on a Sunday.

- Fashion designers who have no shop lay out their wares at the **Kunst-und Handwerkermarkt** (art and craft market), Sat–Sun, in the Strasse des 17 Juni. It complements the flea market, which is held at the same time.
- **Works of art** are on offer Thu–Sun 10–5, in Hinter dem Giesshaus/Am Zeughaus and in Kupfergraben in Berlin-Mitte.
- The finest **covered markets** are the Arminius-Markthalle in Tiergarten, and the hall in Marheinekeplatz in Kreuzberg. Fruit and vegetables, meat and fish, newspapers, household articles and clothing are sold in both.
- The biggest and most popular **weekly markets** are those in Maybachufer (► 142) and in Winterfeldtplatz in Schöneberg (Wed and Sat morning).

Junk and Flea Markets

- **Kunst- und Flohmarkt** (antiques, design, fashion), Strasse des 17. Juni, Sat–Sun 10–5.
- **Allee-Markt** (electronics, art and junk), Karl-Marx-Allee (between the Cosmos cinema and U-Bahn station Weberwiese), Sun noon–6.
- **Trödelmarkt** (junk market), Boxhagener Platz, Sun 9–4.
- **Kunst- und Trödelmarkt Köpenick** (art and junk), Friedrichshagen station, Sun 8–4.
- **Kunst- und Nostalgiemarkt** (books, art, hats), on museum island, at the Zeughaus and in Kupfergraben, Sat–Sun 11–5.
- **Flohmarkt am Arkonaplatz** (flea market), Arkonaplatz, Sun 10–4.
- **Grosser Trödelmarkt Schöneberg** (junk), John-F-Kennedy-Platz, Sat–Sun 8–4.
- **Antik- und Trödelmarkt Steglitz** (antiques and junk), Platz des 4. Juli, Sun 8–4.

Opening Times

- **Normal shop opening times** are Monday to Saturday, 9 or 10 am to 8 pm. Away from the main shopping streets, shops often close at 6 pm. NOTE: shops are normally closed on Sundays (but see below).
- **Small shops** in the tourist centres (Nikolaiviertel, Hackesche Höfe, Prenzlauer Berg) don't open until 11 am or noon.
- **Turkish bakers** in the outskirts often open on Sundays and public holidays as well as normal opening hours.
- On special occasions, like trade fairs and other big events, shops are permitted to open on **Sundays** noon–6.

Entertainment

It's not easy to find out everything that's going on in the city when there are around 3,000 events every day to choose from. Even Berliners can't get by without specific information on what's on offer. For last-minute decisions look in the day's newspaper and this will sometimes tell you what you need to know.

Three large opera houses and several small ones, about 30 theatres and at least as many cabaret theatres, more than a dozen children's theatres, an increasing number of literary salons and readings, some 120 bars and discos, and in summer any number of open-air events and film-showings: if you want to go out you have to be decisive. New comedy clubs keep springing up, pioneered by Kookaburra in Prenzlauer Berg (Schönhauser Allee 184). If you're still trying to decide late into the evening, you can be thankful that midnight is always the right time for dancing, listening to music and many film previews.

Theatre
Berlin's most exciting theatre is the **Volksbühne** in Rosa-Luxemburg-Platz, where a youthful public expects to see spectacular productions, social satire and works by young guest directors. Since Claus Peymann took over Bert Brecht's **Berliner Ensemble** theatre (Bertolt-Brecht-Platz 1), Berlin's finest theatre, audiences are hoping that it will become as famous as the Viennese Burgtheater. The **Deutsche Theater** is highly regarded for the quality of its productions, and the **Schaubühne am Lehniner Platz** (Kurfürstendamm 153), once the most significant theatre in West Germany, is now in the news again with its modern productions. Nor should you forget the countless fringe theatres, puppet and children's theatres, of which the **Grips** in Tiergarten (Altonaer Strasse 22, for over-6s) is the best known.

The Music Scene
Music-lovers go to clubs and bars. More permanent entertainment venues include **Arena** in Eichenstrasse in Treptow, **Columbiahalle** and **ColumbiaFritz** in Platz der Luftbrücke in Tempelhof, **Tempodrom** at Möckernbrücke 10 in Kreuzberg, and **Tränenpalast** in Reichstagsufer in Berlin-Mitte. The classic venue for live concerts and impromptu shows is **Quasimodo**, under the Delphi cinema (Kantstrasse 12a). Live music can also be found at **Junction Bar** (Gneisenaustrasse 18) on weekdays and in the smokey **Yorckschlösschen** (Yorckstrasse 15) on Wednesday evenings and Sunday afternoons.

Looking Around, Drinking, Dancing
If you haven't much time and want an overview of the Berlin scene or just want to people-watch, then go to where there are the most bars: Hackescher Markt in Berlin-Mitte, Oranienstrasse in Kreuzberg, Kollwitzplatz in Prenzlauer Berg, Simon-Dach-Strasse in Friedrichshain. And once you get there? Just go with the flow.

Gays and Lesbians
Berlin is proud of its open gay and lesbian scene. It has left its imprint on **Schöneberg**: in Fuggerstrasse, Eisenacherstrasse and Motzstrasse there are many bars and cafés and rainbow-decorated fast-food stalls (stands). One of the oldest institutions is **Eldorado**, which was already a well-known meeting ground for avant-garde artists in the 1920s. You can find other meeting points

in Gleimstrasse and Greifenhagerstrasse in **Prenzlauer Berg** and in
Oranienstrasse and Mehringdamm in **Kreuzberg**.

Parks

- You don't have to wait till evening to go out in Berlin, especially in
  summer. Public green spaces make up 14.5 per cent of the total area
  of the city, and they are very well used. The centrally placed tiny
  Monbijoupark is in Hackescher Markt. Here workers in their lunch-hour,
  mothers with children and exhausted tourists lie around on the grass.
  There's a small games area, an open-air pool for children and a beach-
  bar with deckchairs on the banks of the Spree.
- The **Volkspark Friedrichshain** is the local park for the students and young
  inhabitants of Prenzlauer Berg and Friedrichshain (U-Bahn station:
  Strausberger Platz). The Café Schönbrunn and the beer garden play
  host to parties long into the night. Apart from the open-air cinema and
  the opportunity to play tennis and basketball, the main attraction is the
  Märchenbrunnen, which in the evening is the focus of one of the
  largest cruising areas in the city.
- When the children who people the **Viktoriapark** during the day are long
  in bed, you can still hear bongo-drum music competing with the
  nightingales. In Golgatha (➤ 152) the night has not yet started, not by
  a long way.

Information

- The information magazines *zitty* and *tip* appear alternately each
  fortnight. For each day they give *Kino* (cinema), *Theater* (theatre) and
  Musikveranstaltungen (concert) programmes, and details of *Lesungen*
  (readings), *Vorträge* (lectures) and parties. There are *Tagestipps* (tips of
  the day) and addresses, with information on *Führungen* (guided tours),
  Märkten (markets), *Kinderveranstaltungen* (children's events), *Kunst* (art)
  exhibitions and much more.
- The **daily papers** also publish details of selected events.
- **Posters** give notice of big events weeks in advance.
- **Theatre box offices** and **ticket agencies** will tell you about current
  performances.

Booking in Advance

- Note that theatre and concert-hall box offices have high advance
  booking charges. **Theatre tickets** can be bought in the Potsdamer Platz
  arcades, at KaDeWe, Karstadt and Wertheim department stores
  (www.showtimetickets.de; free hotline: 0800/88 22 88 22) and in
  almost all areas at stationers' shops.
- You can **order tickets** by phone from most event organisers. These must
  be picked up at least half an hour before the show starts.
- Except for the concerts of the Berlin Philharmonic orchestra, you can
  buy tickets without paying an advance booking charge from **Berlin
  Tourismus Marketing GmbH**, tel: (030) 25 00 25.

Last-Minute Tickets

The agency **Hekticket** often has reduced tickets for same-day events; you'll
find it near Zoo station at Hardenbergstrasse 29d in the foyer (lobby) of the
Deutsche Bank and at Alexanderplatz, Karl-Liebknecht-Strasse 12 – theatre
tel: (030) 24 31 24 31, concerts: (030) 23 09 93 33.

Unter den Linden

Getting Your Bearings

The avenue Unter den Linden is Berlin's high street. It has achieved mythical status because it reflects all the good and bad things that have happened to the country over the centuries. It is not a residential street, nor do Berliners really stroll down it, but they love to show off *die Linden* (the limes) proudly to visitors from the provinces.

Unter den Linden is a daytime street – there's nothing going on at night. Here you can see the Berlin of the Kurfürsten (electoral princes), of the Prussian kings, of the GDR (German Democratic Republic) and also examples of contemporary, if not exciting, architecture. To Berliners it represents Germany's spirit and might. You will find the name is often shortened to "die Linden".

From Pariser Platz with its Brandenburger Tor (Brandenburg Gate) you can see the old Reichstag (parliament building) with its modern glass dome, which is now the seat of the Federal German parliament.

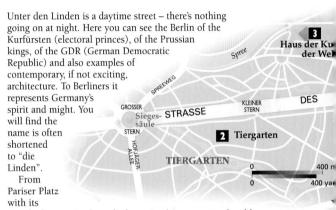

Relaxing under the lime trees

The 21st-century centre of power has developed in the area where the avenue once ended, in the extensive green spaces of the Tiergarten. If you face away from Brandenburger Tor and follow the road down to Schlossplatz, a good kilometre (half a mile) away, you may well be enticed to turn off left or right into Friedrichstrasse.

In the southern reaches of Friedrichstrasse are the Quartieren where you'll find architecturally interesting rows of shops. Crossing the beautiful Gendarmenmarkt and history-laden Bebelplatz you return to Unter den Linden and "Alter Fritz" (Old Fred), the equestrian statue of Frederick the Great under the lime trees.

Page 47: Frederick the Great astride his steed

This broad, tree-lined avenue, with Brandenburger Tor and the Tiergarten, has been the greatest attraction for visitors from East and West since the fall of the Wall in 1989.

Unter den Linden in a Day

9:00 am

People may already be a queueing (lining up) outside the **❶ Reichstag building** (➤ 52–3), but at this hour you have a good chance of getting in to Berlin's number one attraction without waiting too long. From the top of the dome there is a splendid view over the city.

10:00 am

It's still early, and the city is slowly rousing itself. In summer, take a walk through **❷ Tiergarten** (➤ 65) to the **❸ Haus der Kulturen der Welt** (House of World Cultures ➤ 66) on the banks of the Spree.

11:00 am

Stroll back and walk through Brandenburger Tor (Brandenburg Gate), which will bring you to **❹ Pariser Platz** (➤ 54–5). The conference hall of the DG-Bank (left) is well worth a look.

11:30 am

Wander down Unter den Linden and explore first the northern and then the southern end of **❺ Friedrichstrasse** (➤ 56–8). From the lower ground floor of Galeries Lafayette you come to **Quartier 206** (➤ 57), which has fine shops and Venetian marble.

1:30 pm

If appetising smells haven't already tempted you to have a snack in the basement of the Galeries Lafayette, walk to the ❻ **Gendarmenmarkt** (➤ 59–61), which is surrounded by eating places with restful terraces. Pause awhile to admire what is perhaps Berlin's most beautiful square while you eat at the Brasserie am Gendarmenmarkt (➤ 68) or Möhring's (➤ 69).

2:00 pm

Take U-Bahn train U2 one stop to Kochstrasse and Checkpoint Charlie (➤ 56). In the Mauermuseum (Museum of the Wall) you can't fail to admire the courage and imagination of the people who risked their lives to escape from the GDR. Next, walk or take the U-bahn back to Französische Strasse. Follow the street Hinter der Katholischen Kirche down to Bebelplatz, with its memorial to the book-burning carried out by the Nazis in 1933, and to ❷ **Forum Fridericianum** (➤ 62–4), where you'll find the Staatsoper (State Opera), the Neue Wache (New Guardhouse, 1816–18, which holds the tombs of an unknown soldier and an unknown concentration camp victim), Humboldt University and the equestrian statue of Frederick the Great.

6:00 pm

After so much history, you can enjoy a restorative cup of tea in the Tadschikische Teestube (tea room, ➤ 64) with its samovar and deep-pile carpets. Then if you have the energy, cross ❽ **Schlossbrücke** (left; ➤ 67) and admire the statuary or look into the ❾ **Berliner Dom** (cathedral) (➤ 67).

8:00 pm

Something to eat? Stroll back down the central reservation of Unter den Linden to Bocca di Bacco (➤ 68) in Friedrichstrasse or Borchardt's in Gendarmenmarkt (➤ 68). It's wise to book ahead. If what you really want is genuine German food, it's not far away, at Schinkel-Klause (➤ 69).

O Reichstag

In 1995 the Reichstag was wrapped in silvery material by the conceptual artist Christo and his wife Jeanne Claude, forming a monumental image which was seen across the world. Now, the house is the seat of the Federal German Parliament, and it still attracts masses of visitors who are fascinated by the combination of an old building and a modern glass dome. And where else can you walk freely into a parliament building?

The Reichstag, built in 1894, was in its early years the seat of a parliament which was both powerless and hapless under the rule of Kaiser Wilhelm II. The parliament was at least allowed to make decisions about the building, and after 20 years of temporary accommodation they decided on this impressive building in the heart of Berlin. In 1916 Kaiser Wilhelm II had the words *Dem deutschen Volke* (To the German people) inscribed above the entrance. Soon afterwards he had to abdicate, and a member of parliament Philipp Scheidemann declared a republic from a window of the building.

On 27 February, 1933, a fire, the cause of which has never been established, broke out in the Reichstag. The main chamber was destroyed by the fire so parliament could not sit. The Nazi government used this as an opportunity to abolish basic rights, persecute and imprison its opponents and smooth the way for the Third Reich. At the end of World War II Soviet Red Army soldiers hoisted their flag over the ruins. On the same day Hitler committed suicide in his bunker.

First Sitting of the Parliament of a United Germany

The building was rehabilitated in 1961 to enable occassional parliamentary sessions to be held. On 4 October, 1990, the unification of East and West Germany was confirmed by the first sitting of the parliament of a united Germany since the fall of the Wall. The decision was taken to move the Bundestag (German parliament) and the greater part of the Federal government from Bonn to Berlin, and the Reichstag was to be extensively refurbished for use as the parliament house.

Once Christo's silver covering had been removed, British architect Sir Norman Foster's plans for an ultra-modern parliament building were put into action and on 19 April, 1999, the Bundestag held its first sitting here. Controversy surrounded the erection of the

DEM DEUTSCHEN VOLKE

Old and new, beautifully combined

23-m (75-foot) high dome, but nevertheless it immediately became an emblem of Berlin. Two spiral ramps – each 230m (250 yards) long, with a constant slope of 8 degrees – lead you round a tower of 360 mirrors, which direct daylight into the plenary chamber 10m (33 feet) below. At night artificial light shines outwards. Such was the success of Foster's design that he was awarded the Bundesverdienstkreuz (Federal Service Cross).

From the viewing platform at the top of the Bundestag, Brandenburger Tor appears minute. Potsdamer Platz can be picked out by the distinctive emerald green logo on top of the DaimlerChrysler Services tower (➤ 98).

TAKING A BREAK

Head to the upmarket **Dachgarten** restaurant on the Reichstag's roof terrace (open 9–5 and 6:30–midnight, tel: 22 62 99 33). To avoid the queue (line) at the door reserve in advance.

Left: All done by mirrors – daylight in the plenary chamber

🚌 192 A2 ✉ Platz der Republik ☎ Visitor service (only for information on guided tours and events) (030) 22 73 21 52 🕐 Daily 8 am–midnight (last admission 10 pm) 🚇 Unter den Linden 🚌 100 💶 Free

REICHSTAG: INSIDE INFO

Top tips To go on a guided tour of the building or to attend an event in the plenary chamber, you will have to apply in writing to the Besucherdienst des Deutschen Bundestages (Bundestag Visitor Service). You can apply by fax: (030) 22 73 00 27. Give them your phone number and they'll let you know whether the event admits visitors, and if so, when.
• Access to the glass cupola is free, but allow plenty of time if you visit at weekends; the queues (lines) can be long.
• At intervals the dome is closed for cleaning. The roof garden restaurant remains open.

④Pariser Platz

This square has hardly changed in 100 years – apart from the position of the old Brandenburger Tor (Brandenburg Gate). During the Cold War, the gate stood right in the middle of the no man's land along the Wall which had divided Berlin since 13 August, 1961. After the fall of the Wall the construction workers moved in.

When Carl Gotthard Langhans, the city's director of town planning, had the **Brandenburger Tor** built between 1789 and 1791, modelled on the Propylaea (entrance) of the Acropolis in Athens, it was a toll gate marking the western boundary of the historical city and, at the same time, a monument to the might of Prussia. The double portico is supported by 12 Doric columns. At 5.5m (18 feet), the central span was broad enough for royal carriages to pass through – the attendants followed on foot, but the common folk went round the outside. Nowadays the gate is used only for state visits.

In 1957 the East Berlin senate had the damaged gate repaired with stone from Pirna in Saxony, which had been used for its construction 200 years earlier. After reunification the gate spent two years under tarpaulins,

undergoing thorough renovations. Now cars are banned from both the gate and the square.

The **Quadriga** (four-horse chariot) was designed by the Berliner Johann Gottfried Schadow (1764–1850) and executed by the coppersmith Jury, whose niece was the model for Eirene, the goddess of peace, later to become Victoria, the goddess of victory. She was originally naked on the classical model, but that did not please the king and she had to put on a robe before she was allowed to drive the steeds. After the French defeated the Prussians at Jena and Auerstedt in 1806, Napoleon I removed the Quadriga, packing it into 12

The Quadriga aloft

Nauseating

On 30 January, 1933, some 25,000 uniformed followers of Adolf Hitler celebrated his nomination as Chancellor with torch-light processions through Brandenburger Tor. Max Liebermann, the 85-year-old president of the Prussian Academy of Art, watched it from his window and commented: "I can't eat nearly as much as I would like to throw up"

crates and transporting them to Paris. In 1814 the Prussian Marshall Blücher arranged for their return journey, and the square in front of Brandenburger Tor became Pariser Platz.

The City's "Salon"

From 1850 onwards, the baroque façades of the square were simplified on classical lines. It became the emblem of middle-class pride, counter-balancing the castle at the other end of the avenue. Bombs destroyed most of the square in World War II. After the fall of the Wall the town planners sought to re-create the city's "salon" in the empty space. Strict regulations were imposed on the architects: façades had to be made from stone, modelled on the classicism of the 19th century. The American and French embassies, the Academy of Art and the legendary Adlon Hotel – plus a few banks – were rebuilt on their historic sites. In fact, many of the buildings in the square are decidedly modern. In 1997 the Adlon (▶ 38) became the first building to occupy its old site. The **Holocaust Memorial** to the south of the Adlon was designed by the New Yorker Peter Eisenmann.

Left: Night-time at Brandenburger Tor

TAKING A BREAK

Depending on the time of day, **Theodor Tucher's** (Pariser Platz 6a) is a coffee-house, restaurant and reading-room. George W Bush ate here in May 2002.

🔁 192 B2　🚇 Unter den Linden　🚌 100

PARISER PLATZ: INSIDE INFO

Top tips Now and again, the **Liebermann house**, to the left of Brandenburger Tor, plays host to public exhibitions.
• In the northern gate-house there is a **"silent room"**, and in the southern one a tourist information bureau where you can get a plan of the city.

5 Friedrichstrasse

Checkpoint Charlie, the Americans' checkpoint C and border crossing for the Allies, was for decades the best-known spot on Friedrichstrasse. In October 1961 American and Soviet tanks confronted each other here. Today this area is renowned for its elegant shops and luxurious arcades which entice people from across the world into buildings designed by internationally renowned architects.

Haus am Checkpoint Charlie, the museum of the Wall founded in 1962, keeps alive the memory of what life was like during the Cold War; no man's land, fear and daring attempts at escape. (Friedrichstrasse 43–44, tel: (030) 253 72 50, daily 9 am–10 pm, U-Bahn station: Kochstrasse. Admission: expensive).

To the south of Unter den Linden you look down a seemingly unending row of modern buildings; to the north a slight bend in the road obstructs the view to the station and beyond. Friedrichstrasse is 3.3km (2 miles) long. The station of the same name, opened in 1882, divided the street into two unequal parts. To the north it led through industrial

Discrete Style – for Nearly a Mile

Walking from Brandenburger Tor to Friedrichstrasse you may be disappointed with Unter den Linden. What, are *those* the famous lime-trees? It's 1,390 dead-straight metres (1,520 yards) up to the top of this 350-year-old show-piece of classical style. House number 1 was the palace of the Hohenzollern kings and emperors, but it's not there any more – in 1950 the GDR president Grotewohl had the war-damaged historical building blown up with 13,000kg (13 tons) of explosives. The palace is to be rebuilt. After the war, 13 of the original 65 houses under the limes (or parts of them) were still standing. Since then, office buildings have arisen between Pariser Platz and Friedrichstrasse. But the ambassador of the Russian Federation still resides in the Czars' 1832 house, Unter den Linden 63–65.

Checkpoint Charlie – just a reminder

areas, which were later built up with tenements. To the south, as far as Leipzigerstrasse, the buildings were splendidly elegant; the tone was set by de luxe restaurants in cellars, cabarets, night-clubs and amusement arcades with their usual clientele. The journalist Franz Hessel wrote of the "narrow pavement (sidewalk) carpeted with light…, on which dangerous girls moved as though on silk."

After the Wall was built, **Friedrichstrasse station** was the only long-distance and local train connection between East and West; now it is once again a normal U-Bahn and S-Bahn station. To the left, before you get to Weidendamm bridge over the Spree, only the Tränenpalast (meaning literally "palace of tears" – now an arts and entertainments venue) reminds you of the times when people said goodbye in tears at the border crossing here. The scanty buildings continue behind Berliner Ensemble theatre in the direction of Friedrichstadt palace. Before the bridge you can turn right for Museumsinsel (► 78–81).

Friedrichstadt-Passagen

Friedrichstadt-Passagen, a massive develop-ment of office and shopping complexes on the southern reaches of Friedrichstrasse, was built in best Berlin "layer-cake" style (shops below, offices above them, flats at the top) by an international team of architects including IM Pei and Jean Nouvel. **Galeries Lafayette**, a branch of the chic Paris-based department store, on the corner of Französische Strasse marks the start of the blocks known as Quartier 205–207 – it actually occupies 207, an airy structure with a translucent glass cone at its centre.

A stroll through the art deco-style **Quartier 206**, with its angular bays and façades, is enough to drive all thoughts of shopping from your mind. You enter through an atrium which, as soon as you step onto the escalator, opens out and coloured marble mosaics seem to swirl in moving images which might make you dizzy. Dark suits and expensive furs whisk by, snatches of conversations in different languages greet you momentarily, somewhere a piano tinkles, black leather sofas and armchairs invite you to enjoy the show in what is, after all, only a shopping centre, but an exclusive one. Ladies' and mens' fashions, flowers and jewellery are sold in chic outlets, but people for whom designer fashion labels are commonplace shop in Quartier 206 Departmentstore. Only the super-confident would feel at ease here wearing scruffy shoes and carrying a rucksack. At night, American architect Cobb's ribbons of light give a suggestion of the theatre played out behind the façade.

The **Deutsche Guggenheim** museum often puts on interesting exhibitions (Unter den Linden 13–15, tel: (030) 202 09 30, daily 11–8, Thu also 8–10. Admission charge variable, Mon free; free with *SchauLust* pass ➤ 37).

TAKING A BREAK

There are many snack-bars on Friedrichstrasse, but the food department in the basement of **Galeries Lafayette** (➤ 57) is something special.

The splendid atrium of Quartier 206

🔲 192 C1/2   🚇 Friedrichstrasse, Stadtmitte, Französische Strasse

FRIEDRICHSTRASSE: INSIDE INFO

Top tips The Checkpoint Charlie museum (➤ panel, page 56) often has **special exhibitions**, **discussions** and **films**. It's well worth looking at the programme.

Hidden gem Just north of Zimmerstrasse, Mauerstrasse leads to **Bethlehemkirchplatz**, where the outline of the destroyed church of the Bohemian Brothers is sketched out in coloured paving. In the middle stands Claes Oldenbourg's sculpture *Houseball*, based on the sparse goods of the exiled community.

6 Gendarmenmarkt

This is said to be the most beautiful square in Berlin, the very image of Romantic classicism. At the end of a demonstration, tired marchers often rest on the steps of Schinkel's playhouse. The entrance to this concert hall, a former theatre, isn't up the steps, though – it's underneath them.

The square was established in the 17th century as the principal market-place in Friedrichstadt and became a centre for French Huguenot refugees fleeing religious persecution at home. It takes its name from the guardhouse and stables which Friedrich Wilhelm I established here for the *Gens d'armes* regiment. The square already had a small replica of the Huguenots' mother church in Charenton, which served as the French church in Friedrichstadt. As a counterpart to it, the Neue Kirche was built for the German-speaking Swiss immigrants. In 1780, for reasons of symmetry, Friedrich II commissioned Carl von Gontard to add a cupola to each church, thus unwittingly creating the basis for the names they still have: Deutscher and Französischer Dom.

A Coherent Concept

In the **Französischer Dom**, whose lower ground floor has a good restaurant (Refugium) with the finest terrace in the square, there is a Huguenot museum. From the viewing platform you can see that the square was designed as a whole; no building stands by itself. This coherence gives the square its character. In the **Deutscher Dom** the various phases of construction are documented on wall displays, and a permanent exhibition shows the development of parliamentary democracy in Germany.

In the middle of the square, a modest French comedy theatre was replaced in 1802 by Carl Gotthard Langhans's German National Theatre. It lasted only 15 years; during a rehearsal of Schiller's *Die Räuber* the curtain caught fire and the whole house burnt down. The replacement, intended to be the most

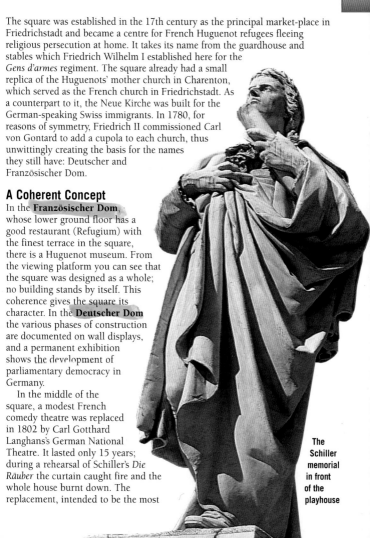

The Schiller memorial in front of the playhouse

modern theatre in Prussia, was designed by
Karl Friedrich Schinkel (▶ panel) in the
Classical style favoured at the time and built
between 1818 and 1821. Sculptures by
Christian Friedrich Tieck adorn the three-
cornered gable above the proscenium arch. In
1945 the SS set fire to the building – post-war
photos show the square as a ploughed field.
The GDR decided to renovate the whole
square and rebuild the theatre, and in 1984 it
was re-opened as a concert hall – at that time
East Berlin already had plenty of theatres. The
Renaissance style of the interior now makes a
splendid setting for many an event.

During World War II the Nazis removed
Reinhold Begas's 6m (20-foot) marble statue of
the dramatist Friedrich Schiller (1759–1805).
Since 1989 it has been restored to its rightful
place, with muses of the arts at its feet: Poetry

Prussia's Star Architect
Karl Friedrich Schinkel
(1781–1841) wanted to be a
painter. He studied at the
Berlin School of Architecture,
but after travelling he worked
as a landscape painter. In
1815 he was appointed to
the Geheimer Baurat (Privy
Counsel for Architecture). He
replanned the whole city
along classical lines. Then he
made a name for himself as
a set-designer. His first
Berlin building was the Neue
Wache (▶ 63) with its Doric
columns, which he designed
when he was 35. The Altes
Museum (▶ 78) is regarded
as his greatest work. His
style is still influential in
Berlin today.

with a harp, Drama with a dagger, Philosophy with a parchment scroll that reads *Erkenne dich selbst* (Know thyself), and History with writing-tablets.

The Centre of the Light-hearted Muse

In the 19th century, Gendarmenmarkt was a cultural and culinary focal point. Johann Strauss, the director of music at the Viennese court, taught Berliners the Viennese waltz, composer Jacques Offenbach invited them, in 1858, to the sumptuous *Bouffes Parisiennes*. Writer ETA Hoffmann was not just a regular customer at Lutter & Wegner's wine bar, he actually lived next door. Rahel Varnhagen invited philosophers, scholars and writers to intellectual discussions at her famous salons in Jägerstrasse, in the house now occupied by Vau's gourmet eatery. The atmosphere must have been rather like it is now, with expensive restaurants and their clientele, bars and entertainment.

At its margins the square doesn't always live up to its classical reputation. Buildings pose architectural puzzles: Is this a new building? Is this one pseudo-classical, or maybe mock Jugendstil (art nouveau)? Sometimes they even have a pinkish tinge, known to those in the trade as *Architecktenmarzipan* (architect's marzipan).

TAKING A BREAK

Fassbender & Rausch serve an excellent authentic hot chocolate, as well as chocolate candies and truffles (Charlottenstrasse 60, Mon–Fri 10–8, Sat 10–5).

Gendarmen-markt – twice as beautiful after a shower

🚇 192 C1/2
🚉 Französische Strasse

Huguenot Museum
☎ (030) 229 17 60 🕐 Tue–Sat 1–5 pm, Sun 11–5 💷 Inexpensive

Deutscher Dom
☎ (030) 22 73 04 31 🕐 Tue 10–10, Wed–Sun 10–6; tours daily 11 am and 1 pm 💷 Free; exhibition free with *SchauLust* pass (➤ 37)

GENDARMENMARKT: INSIDE INFO

Top tips A **peal** of 60 bells is rung daily from the Französischer Dom at noon, 4 pm and 7 pm.
• If you want to have dinner in the Gendarmenmarkt, you'll need to book a table, perhaps at **Borchardt's** (➤ 68).

7 Forum Fridericianum

In the middle of Unter den Linden stands the monument to Friedrich II (Frederick the Great), erected here in 1851. A diverse collection of people is grouped round the base; the fact that the poets are standing under the horse's tail shows how they were ranked at court. Surrounding the statue, Friedrich wanted to build the Forum Fridericianum in his own honour, which is what you see today in Bebelplatz, on the south side of Unter den Linden.

In order to create Forum Fridericianum on his accession in 1740, the 28-year-old Friedrich first had to have Unter den Linden rebuilt. Almost 50 houses had to be demolished, and even then the king didn't have enough room for his official guests. The owners of the mansions had to put some of their suites at the disposal of foreign visitors and also help out by lending their best china, silver and damask tablecloths when there was a banquet at the palace.

The Opera

The architect Knobelsdorff only had time to complete the opera house, in the style of a Corinthian temple (1741–3), before he fell from favour. Officially

called the Staatsoper (State Opera) but known colloquially as the "Lindenoper", it's the most beautiful building on the boulevard and is one of the most visited artistic venues in the city. In its early years this "noblest art", as it was known, was strictly rationed, with performances only in winter, twice a week.

Bebelplatz

On the square the only exception to the otherwise classical framework is the high-baroque exuberance of the **Alte Bibliothek** (Old Library, 1775–80). Its style has earned it the nickname *Kommode* (chest of drawers). It was in fact the king's wish that this copy of the Michaelertrakt in Vienna's Hofburg should stand here. Next to the library stands the **Alte Palais** (Old Palace), in which Kaiser Wilhelm I died in 1888.

On 10 May, 1933, the Nazis burnt 20,000 works of Jewish, pacifist and anti-fascist literature on the square; as a **memorial** to this event the Israeli sculptor Micha Ullmann created subterranean rows of empty bookshelves, which can be seen through a glass panel in the middle of Bebelplatz.

St Hedwig's Cathedral (1773), the only church built under Friedrich II, was a gesture of religious tolerance to the Silesian Catholics; it was modelled, inadequately, on the Roman Pantheon.

Across Unter den Linden stands Humboldt University (by Johann Boumann, 1748–1866), originally planned as a palace for Prince Heinrich, Friedrich's brother. In 1810, on the insistence of Wilhelm von Humboldt, it was put at the disposal of the newly founded university of 300 students. In front of the building, statues of the scholar and his brother Alexander von Humboldt still keep an eye on teaching and research. Max Planck and Albert Einstein taught here, Karl Marx and Karl Liebknecht were students.

The Neue Wache

The Neue Wache (New Guardhouse) next to the university (1816–18) is the prototype of Schinkel's classicism (► panel, page 60). With its enlargement of Käthe Kollwitz's *Pietà*, it has been the central memorial of the Federal Republic since 1993. In GDR times the daily changing of the guard took place in Prussian goose-step before the everlasting flame. In 2003 a former occupant returned to the little chestnut wood between the Wache and the **Maxim-Gorki-Theatre**: the GDR had banished him in 1958 to a park, but now the poet **Heinrich Heine** is back, smiling mischievously under his bronze locks.

The Zeughaus

In 1848, Berliners stormed the Zeughaus (Arsenal) to seize weapons for a republican revolution which was quashed by Friedrich's forces. Originally constructed in 1730, before

Friedrich's time, it was an arsenal until 1875 and a military museum until 1944; rebuilt in 1952 it was the GDR's historical museum and is now the Deutsches Historisches Museum (German Historical Museum). It took until 2003 to build the spectacular extension designed by the Chinese-American architect IM Pei (who was also responsible for the pyramid in the forecourt of the Louvre in Paris).

Taking a break in the Tadschikische Teestube (Tajik tea room)

The Kronprinzen- and Kronprinzessinnenpalais

The 17th-century Kronprinzenpalais (Crown Princes' Palace) opposite the Wache was until around 1840 only a princely town residence. It became famous when the Treaty of Accession of the GDR to the Federal Republic of Germany was signed in its Red Hall on 31 August, 1990. The Kronprinzessinnenpalais (Crown Princesses' Palace) next door also had a quite modest career – it is now the **Operncafé**, offering customers an unbelievable range of cakes, which they can enjoy on its vast terrace.

TAKING A BREAK

On the first floor of the Palais am Festungsgraben behind Neue Wache is the **Tadschikische Teestube** (Tajik tea room). You take your shoes off (no smoking!) and sit on the floor by the samovar (Mon–Fri 5 pm–midnight, Sat–Sun 3 pm–midnight).

Bibliophiles rummage in front of Humboldt University

🕂 192 C2 🚇 100

Deutsches Historisches Museum in the Zeughaus
📮 Unter den Linden 2, Hinter dem Giesshaus 3 ☎ (030) 20 30 40
🕐 Permanent exhibition opens in autumn 2004; temporary exhibition in the new wing daily 10–6 🚉 Hackescher Markt 🚇 100 🎟 Free; exhibition and Pei extension free with *SchauLust* pass (► 37)

FORUM FRIDERICIANUM: INSIDE INFO

Top tip In front of the Humboldt University and in its courtyard there are stalls selling **second-hand books** and old records daily from around 10 am.

At Your Leisure

2 Tiergarten

This green space can be seen from the dome of the Reichstag, stretching on one side down to the Spree, on another to Potsdamer Platz and in the west as far as Zoologischer Garten station – 200ha (almost 500 acres) in all. Once the hunting-ground of Electoral Princes, it is Berlin's most important park; in July it hosts the Love Parade (▶ 17). Under Friedrich I, in the first half of the 17th century, a road was built across the park, which is now Strasse des 17. Juni, joining the city to the newly built Schloss Charlottenburg (▶ 120-2). The Grosser Stern (then Kurfürstenplatz), where eight roads meet to form a star, was also constructed at that time. Frederick

It's Great to Be Here

The Tiergarten is the place for tired sightseers to relax and rest their weary feet. In the Café am Neuen See (▶ 69) you can not only eat and drink, but also hire a boat. Throughout the park you'll see people strolling, sunning themselves, reading, playing games, running, cycling or picnicing. In the north of the park, the Spree passenger steamers stop at the Haus der Kulturen der Welt (House of World Cultures, ▶ 66).

the Great commissioned his architect Knobelsdorff to lay out a pleasure park. The fence surrounding the hunting-ground was removed and the square ringed with statues which the populace, who were now permitted to walk there, christened *Puppen* (puppets, dolls). To the south mazes were constructed, to the east there was soon a whole network of paths, so

18th-century Berliners had a real place to relax.

In 1939 the Siegessäule (victory column) was moved from Königsplatz (now Platz der Republik) to the Grosser Stern. It was erected in 1873 to commemorate Prussia's victories over Denmark (1864), Austria (1866) and France (1870–1). It is topped by the 35-ton, 8.3m (27-foot) high statue

Enjoying the Love Parade beneath the Siegessäule

of Viktoria, the goddess of victory. After climbing 285 steps up the spiral staircase you reach the 48m (157-foot) high viewing platform, below the goddess's flowing bronze skirt.

World War II wrought destruction on the former splendours of the Tiergarten. In the post-war years trees and bushes were taken for

Haus der Kulturen der Welt below its spectacular roof

firewood, and potatoes and vegetables were planted instead of flowers. Since 1949, replanting has restored the landscape. The Englischer Garten (English Garden), between the Bundespräsident's (Federal President's) Schloss Bellevue and Altonaer Strasse, also stems from that time. The trees near the palace conceal a black oval building, the Bundespräsident's new office.

✚ 195 D5–F4 ⊕ Aussichtsplattform Mon 1–5:30, Tue–Sun from 9 am 🚌 100 💷 Inexpensive

❸ Haus der Kulturen der Welt

In the middle of the 18th century two Huguenots set up tents in the Tiergarten to sell drinks; this soon became a favourite destination for an outing. Controversy was aroused when during the March 1848 revolutionary political meetings were held "In den Zelten" ("In the tents", still the name of a street). Since the 1957 international architectural exhibition the site on the banks of the Spree has been occupied by a gift from the Americans, a conference hall which Berliners immediately named *schwangere Auster* (pregnant oyster); part of the roof, a daringly constructed concrete tent, collapsed in summer 1980. The damage was repaired in 1987 for the city's 750-year jubilee. Since 1989 it has been the Haus der Kulturen der Welt (House of World Cultures), a striking building which houses exhibitions, conferences and other events on every aspect of world culture. At the foot of the terrace there is a jetty for boat trips on the Spree. In the pool in front of the hall stands Henry Moore's sculpture *Two Forms*. A peal of 68 bells is rung each day from the 42m (138-foot) high bell-tower.

✚ 195 F5 ✉ John-Foster-Dulles-Allee ☎ (030) 394 86 79, www.hkw.de 🚌 100

The Soviet War Memorial

On Strasse des 17. Juni, near Brandenburger Tor, stands the Soviet war memorial, erected in 1945. The entrance is flanked by two T34 tanks, the first to enter the city in April 1945. The colonnade is made from granite blocks taken from the destroyed Neue Reichskanzlei (New Chancellery). As a sign that the war is over, the 8m (26-foot) high Red Army soldier has his rifle slung over his shoulder. Some 2,500 soldiers killed in action in Berlin are buried in the memorial.

8 Schlossbrücke

You can see at a glance that the name Marx-Engels-Brücke doesn't suit this bridge, even if that was what it was called in GDR times. When Karl Friedrich Schinkel designed it between 1819 and 1824, he was fulfilling the wishes of Friedrich Wilhelm III by replacing the dilapidated "dog-bridge", so called because hunters would set out from here with their hounds. The replacement was to be distinguished, adorning the site but also radiating dignity. Schinkel died in 1841, and his sculptures were not put up until the reign of Friedrich Wilhelm IV. Standing with the equestrian statue of Frederick the Great behind you, the themes of the corner groups show Nike, goddess of victory, from left to right: teaching a boy heroic legends, crowning the victor, supporting a wounded soldier, and bearing the dead warrior up to Olympus. The central group shows a young man receiving weapon training, being given his weapons and led into battle and protected. Berliners were greatly shocked: the groups were all naked!

⊞ 193 D2   🚌 100

9 Berliner Dom

Seelengasometer (soul gasometer) was what Berliners disparagingly called the ornate, neo-baroque cathedral with which Kaiser Wilhelm II replaced its too modest predecessor on the banks of the Spree.

The imperial client had in mind something along the lines of St Peter's in Rome, to be the leading church of German Protestantism and burial place of the Hohenzollern rulers. Julius Raschdorff's design was inspired by the Italian high Renaissance. The massive central dome is 74.8m (245 feet) high and richly ornamented, with additional towers at each corner. Reconstruction of the war-damaged building began in 1975, and in 1993 it was re-opened with a solemn service.

The sarcophaguses of the Great Elector and his wife Dorothea and of the first royal couple Friedrich I and Sophie Charlotte are in the nave, as is the tomb of Kaiser Friedrich III; the tombs of the Hohenzollerns of the 16th to 20th century are on view in the Hohenzollern vault. Berliner Dom was the first church in the city to charge visitors for admission.

⊞ 193 D2   ✉ Lustgarten   🕐 Daily 8–8   🚌 100   💲 Moderate

The ornate Berliner Dom

Where to...
Eat and Drink

Prices

Prices given are for one person, excluding drinks.

€ under 12 euros €€ 12–25 euros €€€ over 25 euros

RESTAURANTS

Bocca di Bacco €€€

There's no lack of eateries around Gendarmenmarkt nor of Italians in Berlin, but Bocca di Bacco (Mouth of Bacchus) is the gastronomic high point of the area. The large restaurant is simply but elegantly furnished. The cuisine is North Italian, the ingredients are outstandingly fresh, and the menu will satisfy vegetarians too.

➕ 192 C1 🗺 Friedrichstrasse 167/168 ☎ (030) 20 67 28 28 🕐 Mon–Sat noon–midnight, Sun 6–midnight

Borchardt €€

When in 1853 August Friedrich Wilhelm Borchardt opened his wine bar in the 200sq m (240-square yard) former assembly rooms of the Huguenot community near Gendarmenmarkt, in order to bring a more cosmopolitan element to the provincial capital, he little thought that this same bar would become one of the most famous and most popular restaurants in the city. The restaurant has long been known as the politicians' and media people's canteen. It is always fresh and always good. The *crème brûlée* delicately flavoured

with lemon grass is said to be the best in town.

➕ 192 C2 🗺 Französische Strasse 47 ☎ (030) 20 38 71 10 🕐 Daily 11 am–1 am

Brasserie am Gendarmenmarkt €€

With its dark wood, chrome and neo-art-deco ambience, this is a really good brasserie for anyone who wants a "Quick-Lunch" – three courses in half an hour. Both at lunch-time and in the evening freshly cooked Italian, French and German dishes are served by friendly waiters. In the afternoon there's less of a squash on the red benches, and you can enjoy the terrace on Gendarmenmarkt.

➕ 192 C1 🗺 Taubenstrasse 30 ☎ (030) 20 45 35 01 🕐 Daily 11:30–1 am, Quick-Lunch 11:30–4

Die Möwe €€

In GDR times the Möwe was a well-known artists' club, and it still has something of this atmosphere. The

austere rooms have high ceilings, and the piano and the red seats remind one of a saloon. The cuisine has a French bias. On Monday evenings, when there's a two-course menu, with cabaret, readings or satirical songs, it's particularly advisable to book.

➕ 192 C2 🗺 Palais am Festungsgraben 1 ☎ (030) 20 61 05 40 🕐 Mon–Sat 6–midnight

Einstein €–€€

This is more than a café in a wonderful position, where you can enjoy a sandwich or bagel sitting on the central strip of Unter den Linden, looking at Brandenburger Tor. In the restaurant, Austrian cuisine of remarkably good quality is served.

➕ 192 B2 🗺 Unter den Linden 42 ☎ (030) 204 36 32 🕐 Daily 7 am–1 am

issan €–€€

Above a door opposite the Adlon hotel (▶ 38) is a sign saying *Kleines*

Restaurant (Little Restaurant), and indeed it is so small that you could easily miss it. The furnishing is simple, the service extremely welcoming and the Thai cooking outstanding. The menu of the day – soup and main course – is delicious coconut-milk soups and grilled prawns. Under the thatched roof of the bar, exotic thirst-quenching drinks are served.

+ 192 B2 ⊠ **Unter den Linden 78** ☎ **(030) 22 48 81 47** Ⓖ **Mon–Fri noon–3, 6–11, Sat 6–11**

Schinkel-Klause €–€€ ✏

Visitors from far and wide have heard there's a place serving typical Berlin dishes, *Eisbein* (knuckle of pork), *Königsberger Klopsen* (meatballs) and perhaps even proper tureens of soup, but they look for it in vain among all the Japanese, Italian and French restaurants. You can find it in the basement of the

Kronprinzessinnenpalais (➤ 64), under the Operncafé. Appropriate sculptures and pictures decorate the place. The seating is comfortable, the service welcoming and the cuisine, including vegetarian dishes, is really good, not just substantial.

+ 197 D5 ⊠ **Unter den Linden 5** ☎ **(030) 20 26 84 50** Ⓖ **Daily from 11:30 am**

Ständige Vertretung €–€€

This is a remnant of the former Federal capital Bonn, a place for homesick Rhinelanders, with walls covered with large-format pictures depicting the country's political history. Berliners accept that here you sit very, very close together and drink *Kölsch* (Cologne) lager out of "test-tubes" – what else can you call the minute vessels in which the top-fermented beer is served? The best thing on the menu is the *Flammekuchen*, a wafer-thin pizza served on a wooden board

with various tasty savoury or sweet toppings.

+ 192 B3 ⊠ **Schiffbauerdamm 8** ☎ **(030) 282 39 65** Ⓖ **Daily 11 am–1 am**

CAFÉS

Café am Neuen See

Imagine breakfasting until 4 pm, sitting in the beer-garden by the water or, in autumn and winter, sitting inside looking out it too. No matter whether it's an Italian breakfast with a variety of sausages and cheese, or an Atlantic spread (salmon, halibut), or muesli, you can gather your strength here to face the day or afternoon. It's very full at weekends, but in summer there's always room in the large beer-garden. From midday on there's a mouth-watering selection of pizzas.

+ 195 D4 ⊠ **Lichtensteinallee 2** ☎ **(030) 254 49 30** Ⓖ **Daily 10–10; Sat–Sun 10–10, Nov–Feb Mar–Oct; Sat–Sun 10–10, Nov–Feb**

Möhring ✏

An institution in its former site on Kurfürstendamm, Möhring has now followed the trend and moved to Berlin-Mitte. Many regular customers are here in the week, enjoying the discreet art deco ambience. Breakfast is served at any time, but try to fit in the really delicious cakes.

+ 192 C1 ⊠ **Charlottenstrasse 55** ☎ **(030) 203 09 22 40** Ⓖ **Daily 8 am–midnight**

Operncafé

Delicate little chairs and palms, just as you would imagine an opera café, decorate this former princesses' palace. Individual pots of coffee are served with a choice of 140 different cakes. But you're also well provided for if you want something more substantial. In summer there's plenty of room on the terrace.

+ 197 D5 ⊠ **Unter den Linden 5** ☎ **(030) 20 26 83** Ⓖ **Daily 8 am–midnight**

Where to... Shop

Unter den Linden is not a shopping street. On the first stretch from Pariser Platz you can buy picture postcards and chunks of the Wall, but for real shopping the best places are the Friedrichstadt-Passagen in Friedrichstrasse (▶ 57–8).

FRIEDRICHSTRASSE

The southern end of fashionable Friedrichstrasse down to Leipziger Strasse is one uninterrupted shopping mile, where everything luxurious and expensive is to be found, from fountain-pens (Mont Blanc) to hand-sewn shoes (Budapester) to deliciously irresistible confectionery. All the well-known designer labels are available in the **Friedrichstadt-Passagen**. Many of the goods on sale in Quartier 206 Departmentstore would save you the journey to New York's Fifth Avenue. Cheaper ones are also available, to tempt less wealthy customers.

At the northern end of Friedrichstrasse, **Dussmann's** (Friedrichstrasse 90) campaigns for unlimited opening times and sets the example itself: books and music, snacks and computers can be bought from Monday to Saturday from 10 am to 10 pm. In the **Georgenstrasse antique market** under the railway arches next to Friedrichstrasse station some 60 traders display a variety of wares from various epochs.

TIERGARTEN/ STRASSE DES 17. JUNI

A junk and art market is held on Strasse des 17. Juni by Tiergarten S-Bahn station every Saturday and Sunday from 10 am to 5 pm.

Where to be... Entertained

UNTER DEN LINDEN

In the evening the area around Gendarmenmarkt and Unter den Linden is pretty quiet. Anyone going out here is on their way to the **Staatsoper** (Unter den Linden 5–7, tel: (030) 20 35 45 55), which has become Berlin's leading musical venue with its chief conductor Daniel Barenboim, to the **Komische Oper** (Behrenstrasse 55–57, tel: (030) 47 99 74 00) or to the **Konzerthaus am Gendarmenmarkt** (tel: (030) 203 09 21 01). The **Maxim-Gorki-Theater** behind the Neue Wache (Am Festungsgraben 2, tel: (030) 20 22 11 29) puts on not only Russian playwrights but also contemporary works by American and German authors. **Cookies**, a club legend, which has moved again and again, is on the corner of Unter den Linden and Charlottenstrasse.

FRIEDRICHSTRASSE

Behind Friedrichstrasse station, bars and higher culture mix. **Berliner Ensemble** theatre (tel: (030) 28 40 81 55) made first Bertolt Brecht and then Heiner Müller famous. Events at the **Tränenpalast** (▶ 57; tel: (030) 206 10 00) range from cabaret to jazz. Bus-loads of spectators regularly roll up to the **Friedrichstadtpalast** (tel: (030) 23 26 23 26), a gigantic revue theatre. At 1 pm every Sunday the **Kalkscheune** (tel: (030) 59 00 43 40) puts on Dr Seltsams Fruhschoppen (cabaret).

Spandauer Vorstadt

Getting Your Bearings

English, Spanish and French are widely spoken in Spandauer Vorstadt, a meeting-place for young people from across the world looking to bring some excitement into their lives. They want their imaginations to be stimulated by the mystical and their future to be uncertain and enigmatic.

This district is often called the *Scheunenviertel* (Barns Quarter), but this is historically inaccurate; the district where there were barns on the outskirts of the city in the 17th century, and where poor members of the Jewish community from the East later lived, was in fact further east, where Volksbühne and Rosa-Luxemburg-Platz are now. Perhaps the

The gleaming golden dome of the synagogue

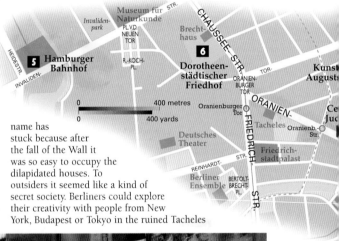

name has stuck because after the fall of the Wall it was so easy to occupy the dilapidated houses. To outsiders it seemed like a kind of secret society. Berliners could explore their creativity with people from New York, Budapest or Tokyo in the ruined Tacheles

Page 71:
Street life in Hackesche Höfe

Tacheles:
Tuning up and chilling out

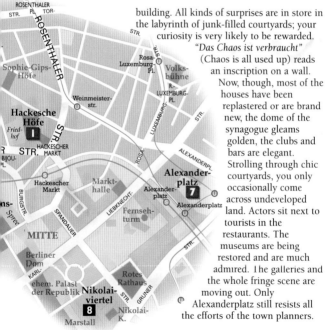

building. All kinds of surprises are in store in the labyrinth of junk-filled courtyards; your curiosity is very likely to be rewarded. *"Das Chaos ist verbraucht"* (Chaos is all used up) reads an inscription on a wall. Now, though, most of the houses have been replastered or are brand new, the dome of the synagogue gleams golden, the clubs and bars are elegant. Strolling through chic courtyards, you only occasionally come across undeveloped land. Actors sit next to tourists in the restaurants. The museums are being restored and are much admired. The galleries and the whole fringe scene are moving out. Only Alexanderplatz still resists all the efforts of the town planners.

★ Don't Miss

At Your Leisure

Until recently it was grey, crumbling and scheduled for demolition, but now Spandauer Vorstadt is youthful, bright and becoming ever more fashionable. No district of Berlin has changed so much and so fast since reunification.

Spandauer Vorstadt in a Day

10:00 am

It is not too early to have a cappuccino or a latte macchiato in the courtyards of the **❶ Hackesche Höfe** (courtyards, ➤ 76–7). There's nothing much doing yet, the first shops (left) are just opening. Apart from in the evening, this is the best time to be here.

10:30 am

There are five museums close together on **❷ Museumsinsel** (Museum Island, ➤ 78–81). To make it easier for you to choose, some of the museums are closed for renovation until 2010.

1:00 pm

Walk along beside the arches of the S-Bahn and find yourself a good place for lunch in one of the restaurants.

2:00 pm

Crossing Montbijou Park you arrive in Oranienburger Strasse. To the left you see the shining golden dome of the new synagogue in the **❸ Centrum Judaicum** (➤ 82–3). It's worth picking up an acoustic guide at the entrance. You'll learn more about the district here than anywhere else.

4:00 pm

Close by, only one U-Bahn stop from the 5 **Hamburger Bahnhof** (➤ 86) is a remarkable gallery, the 4 **Kunstwerke Auguststrasse** (left, ➤ 86). Alternatively, for relaxation, you could go to Friedrichbrücke (Burgstrasse) and take a boat trip under some of the bridges of the Spree. Children love it too.

5:30 pm

If you have an afternoon coffee up in the rotating panorama-level café of the television tower (right) in **Alexanderplatz** (➤ 84–5) the whole town will move past you in half an hour. If that's too fast, just enjoy the view from the platform.

6:30 pm

Spandauer Strasse runs between the Rotes Rathaus (right, ➤ 84) and the 8 **Nikolaiviertel** (➤ 87). End your day where Berlin began, or go one stop on the S-Bahn to Hackesche Markt, glance into the many small shops and start your evening's entertainment with a good meal.

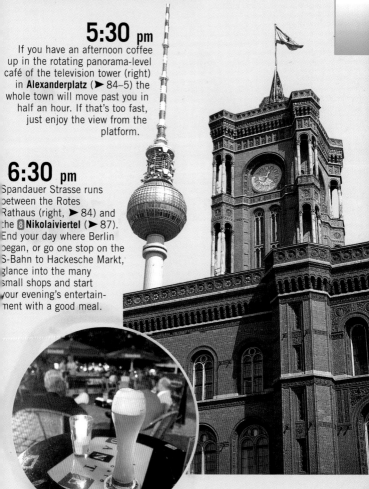

⓪ Hackesche Höfe

Unexpected entrances lead from noisy streets into this network of quiet courtyards – a typical pattern in Berlin. But it's not at all typical for the curious visitor to be greeted by such a magnificent scene.

Right: An open courtyard in a peaceful residential area

A picture-book courtyard

From outside you get no hint of the golden, green and blue clinker bricks (copies of traditional models), high windows, striking patterns and curving roof-lines that draw curious passers-by like a magnet from Rosenthaler Strasse into Hackesche Höfe.

This complex comprising eight interlinked courtyards was built by the renowned architect August Endell. He designed the buildings in art deco style at the start of the 20th century, when the economy was flourishing and the price of building land in the city had rocketed making space at a premium. The complex is situated near the Stadtschloss (City Palace) and the shopping area, between Rosenthaler Strasse and Sophienstrasse. The optimal use of space, the combination of residential and commercial properties and, naturally, the beauty of the first courtyard, all immediately attracted the attention of potential tenants.

Off the Beaten Track

In the courtyard of Rosenthaler Strasse 39, right next to Hackesche Höfe, a narrow stairway leads up the side of the building to **Blindenwerkstatt Otto Weidt**. Here visually impaired Jewish and non-Jewish Berliners survived the Nazi period making brooms and brushes in what was termed an "essential occupation" (Mon–Fri noon–8, Sat–Sun 11–8, admission inexpensive).

A New Way of Living

At a time when flats in Berlin tenements held six to thirteen people, these apartments had central heating, parquet flooring, bathrooms, inside toilets and balconies. The occupants came from middle-class and official circles. Many had shops and workshops in the courtyards. There were producers of textiles,

elephones and liquor, as well
as an oilcloth factory, furriers
and cobblers. Of the 179
members of the Jewish
community who lived and
worked here in 1939, not one
remained in 1944.

After the World War II the
courtyards were neglected,
and were used as workshops
and storehouses. In 1961 the stucco facings
were removed. Immediately after the fall of the
Wall, a society was founded which has done
much to ensure that Hackesche Höfe
are as beautiful today as when they were
built and that their existing character will
be protected.

For Kids
In **Montbijou Park** you'll
find children's playgrounds,
and from the jetty by
Friedrichsbrücke you can
explore the riverside city
centre by boat. In the
Heckmann courtyards
(Oranienburger Strasse 32)
there's a sweet factory where
you can visit the kitchen
(Wed–Sun, from noon).

Promotion of Urban Life
In 1995, after the lavish
renovation of Hackesche Höfe,
the Berlin Senate, the
business proprietors and
the tenants worked out a
scheme for the promotion of urban life which lays down
that all restaurants and shops must be run by their
owners. It also stipulates that the mixed usage of the
courtyards – flats, offices, culture, workshops and eateries
– should remain, with varied rents.

The former ballrooms are now used for variety shows.
Right at the top, under the roof there's a cinema and a bar.
Fashion designers develop their creations, you can watch
goldsmiths at work, and in Brunnenhof a gallery hosts
exhibitions. You can hire bicycles, listen to Yiddish music,
visit an architectural gallery, buy new and second-hand books
– or just look around.

TAKING A BREAK
There are great places to sit everywhere within the courtyards, especially
outside in summer.

✚ 193 D3 ✉ Rosenthaler Strasse 40/41 Ⓗ Hackescher Markt

HACKESCHE HÖFE: INSIDE INFO

Top tip Leave through Hof (Courtyard) VI and you come to Sophienstrasse.
Turn left and walk down to the entrance on the right of the **Sophie-Gips-Höfen**
(Sophie Plasterwork Courtyards) (No 21), which house an art collection.
There are other fine courtyards in Oranienburger Strasse 27 and 32.

One to miss Since 2002, Rosenthaler Strasse has been connected to
Hackesche Höfe by the **Rosenhöfe**, a confection of pink and turquoise
façades and dainty balconies.

2 Museumsinsel

There are more than 150 museums in Berlin, so why visit thes in particular? Because the Altes Museum is housed in one of the finest and for its time most daring buildings. Because the Alte Nationalgalerie, now immaculately restored, has an outstanding collection. And because the Pergamonmuseum is quite rightly the most visited in Berlin.

Approaching Museumsinsel (Museum Island) from the direction of Hackescher Markt, pause for a while on Friedrichsbrücke; there's plenty to see. Tour-boats pass below on the Spree; half their passengers will be Berliners, always on the lookout to see what has changed in their city. The westbound S-Bahn rattles across the river, and the golden dome of the **synagogue** (➤ 82) shines out from Oranienburger Strasse. An accordion or saxophone may be playing – everywhere in Berlin you'll hear accomplished Russian orchestral players who can't find employment back home. Sparrows twitter noisily in the trees in front of the showy Berliner Dom (➤ 67), and you may see people setting up the lighting for a film backdrop.

Altes Museum
Enter the Altes Museum (Old Museum) from the front, from the Lustgarten. Architect Karl Friedrich Schinkel designed the museum, the first to be built on the island, in the early 19th century. He wanted to complement the large palace for the Hohenzollern kings that stood nearby (the palace was severely

For the Improvement of Taste

We have the archaeologist Alois Hirt to thank for the fact that a museum was built here at all. In 1797 he considered that, for the betterment of taste in general and the lot of artists in particular, the best objects in the royal collections should be brought together. However, compared with other courtly collections, there wasn't much to assemble. In the nick of time the English timber merchant Solly offered a remarkable collection for 500,000 Taler; in addition, the Giustiniani Collection in Paris, with its Italian early baroque pieces and works by Caravaggio, was for sale. Friedrich Wilhelm III dipped into his private purse, and when in 1830, on the king's birthday, Schinkel's museum was officially opened, 1,198 paintings were on show.

Left: The Altes Museum, as noble as the Pantheon

damaged during World War II and was torn down in 1950), the cathedral and the arsenal with a meeting-place for the citizens of Berlin. Visitors climb the broad stairway leading up to an open, columned hall, designed on the Greek model – a temple of the arts. They were to be "uplifted" (as Schinkel put it) in the rotunda, inspired by the Pantheon in Rome, before going on to see the collections. Twenty Corinthian columns support the circular gallery of the two-storey domed hall.

The museum holds a splendid collection of antiquities. The most important work in the collection is the **Praying Boy** from Rhodes, sculpted in 300 BC and standing now exactly where it stood when the museum was opened in 1830, in the middle of the North Hall.

Alte Nationalgalerie

The Alte Nationalgalerie (Old National Gallery; 1866–76), designed by Friedrich August Stüler, stands like a Corinthian temple behind Schinkel's museum – up on its high plinth, removed from everyday life below it. At the entrance, visitors are received by the Prussian king Friedrich Wilhelm IV on his steed. The gallery owes its existence to a resolute patron, the banker Joachim Wagener. He had bought Schinkel's Gothic painting **Cathedral on the Sea** and various smaller genre paintings and bequeathed his collection to Kaiser Wilhelm I on condition that it be used to found a national gallery for

A place to rest at the feet of the Amazon warrior

Prussian Cultural Property

Land Preussen (the state of Prussia) was abolished on 25 February, 1947, by Law No 46 of the Allied Control Commission. Its art treasures belonged from then on to the victors in World War II. The Soviet Union allowed the GDR to keep most of its share; in the West the Stiftung Preusslicher Kulturbe (Foundation for Prussian Cultural Property) was founded in 1957, with its seat in Berlin. Within the terms of the treaty of unification it was decided to bring the collections and museums together under the title of Staatliches Museen zu Berlin – Preussischer Kulturbesitz. So works of art are still on the move.

contemporary art in an "appropriate venue". After the bourgeois revolution of 1848, many artists and liberal politicians thought that it was for the state to care for this collection.

The gallery re-opened in 2001 after careful renovation. This shrine to German national culture has become an international collection of 19th-century art. Seventeen works by Caspar David Friedrich, the great artist of Romanticism, are on show, along with 70 by the Berliner Adolph Menzel and 18 by Max Liebermann, but there are also three works by Renoir, four by Claude Monet and works by sculptors ranging from Reinhold Begas to Rodin.

Right: The Pergamon Altar tells of the deeds of heroes

Neues Museum

The "New Museum" was reputed to be the most beautiful of the museums and it was the most severely damaged in World War II. It was re-opened briefly in autumn 2000, then again in summer 2001, and then only for a few weeks. Originally, Stüler's museum (1834–47), with its cast iron work, new building materials and paints, ceiling papers and built-in oriental objects, was itself a work of art. In future – perhaps by 2009 – it will become an Egyptian museum with collections of papyri.

Like a mighty ship the Bodemuseum towers over the water

Pergamonmuseum

Having mounted the 27 steps of Berlin's most exciting stairway, you find yourself standing in front of the ***Telephos Frieze*** from the Pergamon Altar. This historical picture book shows the unwanted birth of Telephos, the mythical founder of the ancient city of Pergamon, his exposure on the hillside, his journey as a growing boy to Asia Minor, his first heroic deeds, the reunion of mother and son, the death of his wife on the battlefield, the Amazon Hiera, and finally his wounding and cure.

The Pergamon Altar, one of the seven wonders of antiquity, is the main attraction of the museum, the most recent of the buildings to be constructed on Museumsinsel. The altar has been a magnet to the public ever since the museum opened in 1930. Built in the 2nd century AD, the altar was discovered by German engineer Carl Humann on the west coast of Turkey in 1878. He spent eight years disinterring it and then had it shipped to Berlin. The museum has other breathtaking, gigantic items such as the **market gate from Miletus** in Ionia, the **Ishtar gate**, the **Babylonian processional road** and the **Mshatta facade**.

Bodemuseum

This neo-baroque museum of Byzantine art, which has towered like a ship's prow over the water since 1904, is not expected to re-open until 2006.

TAKING A BREAK

All the museums have a café for their exhausted visitors.

The Temple City on the Internet

In 1999 Museuminsel was declared a World Cultural Heritage Site by UNESCO, but this tourist magnet will remain a building site until 2010. Only on the internet can visitors move, as though with X-ray eyes, through a 3-D image of the houses and take a virtual walk through the underground archaeological promenade which will, in future, link all the museums. www.museuminsel-berlin.de

➕ 193 D2/3 ✉ Museumsinsel ☎ (030) 20 90 50 🕐 Tue–Sun 10–6, Alte Nationalgalerie Thu until 10 pm 🚇 Hackescher Markt, Friedrichstrasse 🚌 100 💵 Moderate

MUSEUMSINSEL: INSIDE INFO

Top tips The **Tageskarte (day-ticket)** is valid for all Staatlichen Museen (state museums) on one day. Admission is also free with *SchauLust* pass (▶ 37)
• On the first Sunday of the month **admission is free**.

3 Centrum Judaicum

The golden dome of the Neue Synagoge (New Synagogue) in Oranienburger Strasse dominates the sky over Spandauer Vorstadt. Police patrol in front of it, a sign of the continuing danger to which Jewish institutions are exposed.

The synagogue, constructed between 1988 and 1995, is not new in the true sense. A small prayer room and some architectural fragments remain as evidence of the beauty of the original synagogue and its violent destruction. Photos, original documents and recorded reminiscences recall Berlin Jewish life as it used to be.

Preserved and Yet Destroyed

Schinkel's pupil Eduard Knoblauch had in mind the Moorish Alhambra in Granada when he designed the original building in the mid-19th century. In the *Kristallnacht* (Night of Broken Glass) of 9 November, 1938, when many Jewish properties were attacked by the SA ("brown-shirts"), a courageous policeman prevented the destruction of this Moorish-Byzantine masterpiece, saying that it was a listed building. But bombs from a British air raid in November 1943 reduced it to a ruin, which was finally demolished in 1958.

Waiting to Emigrate

In 1933 there were 173,000 members of the Jewish community living in Berlin. By summer 1945 only 8,000 were left, many of whom were waiting for permission to emigrate. The Nazis had deported and murdered more than 55,000 Jewish Berliners, and the rest were forced to emigrate.

The Largest Jewish Community in Germany

At its inauguration the synagogue was capable of holding a congregation of 3,200, but such a large place of worship is no longer needed. With its 12,000 members, the Jewish community of Berlin is admittedly the largest in Germany, but many of the new arrivals, mostly from the former Soviet Union, have as yet to take full advantage of its facilities. The Centrum Judaicum offers them an archive and rooms for assemblies, teaching and study, exhibitions and prayer. With its community hall, library, further education college and the Oren

**Right:
Neighbours
new and the
old in
Oranienburger
Strasse**

restaurant, it has created a new centre of Jewish life.

Grass and Stones

If you turn off Oranienburger Strasse into Grosse Hamburger Strasse you come to a stretch of lawn. The Jewish old people's

In the Oren restaurant

home, which stood here, was the central assembly point for Jewish Berliners before they were deported to concentration camps. Since 1984 a group of sculptures by Willi and Mark Lammert keeps its memory alive. Opposite the sculptures, names written on the fire-blackened walls commemorate the occupants of a bombed-out building. An inconspicuous grass area on the corner of Oranienburger Strasse had been the first Jewish cemetery in the city, dating from 1672, until it was destroyed and levelled in 1943. Since 1998 a single gravestone has stood there, marking the spot where the grave of Moses Mendelssohn, the philosopher and founder of a creative dynasty, is thought to lie.

**Left: The Neue
Synagoge was
formerly the
symbol of a
self-confident
Jewish middle-
class**

TAKING A BREAK

The kosher **Beth Café** in Tucholskystrasse serves light meals.

➕ 192 C3 ✉ Oranienburger Strasse 28 ☎ (030) 88 02 83 00 🕒 Sun–Thu 10–6, Fri 10–2 🚇 Hackescher Markt, Oranienburger Tor 💷 Expensive

---

CENTRUM JUDAICUM: INSIDE INFO

Top tips The **Hof-Theater** at Hackesche Höfe 11 puts on Yiddish plays or concerts every day.
• At Auguststrasse 77 is the **kosher food store** of the orthodox community Adass Jisroel.

Hidden gem If you ask, you may be allowed to visit the gilded **dome** of the Neue Synagoge. Photography is not permitted, however, because of the potential safety risk. The climb to the top is worthwhile – there's a fine view over the old centre of Berlin.

⑦ Alexanderplatz

This vast square was the focal point of East Berlin before the fall of the Wall. It has also been a popular place to hold demonstrations. The Fernsehturm (television tower), the highest building in Berlin, lies at its heart, and can be seen from practically any place in the city.

The square, known affectionately as "Alex" to Berliners, was badly damaged by Allied bombs during World War II. When it was rebuilt, it became a showcase for GDR architecture, looming, unattractive examples of which now surround it. There are ambitious plans to revamp the square, following the designs submitted by Berlin architect Hans Kohlhoff.

The best way to see the square is to have yourself whisked to the top of the **Fernsehturm**, which will take 40 seconds. The 368m (1,207-foot) high structure has long been an icon for all Berlin.

St Walter

On the completion of the television tower in 1969 it was discovered that when the sun shone on the globe at the top a silvery cross appeared, which even Walter Ulbricht, head of the GDR Communist Party, was powerless to correct. The tower was nicknamed St Walter.

The square below used to be a (cattle) market and parade ground. When in 1805 Czar Alexander I visited Friedrich Wilhelm III, it was renamed in his honour. From then on it gradually became a traffic intersection. At that time the 13th-century **Marienkirche** (Our Lady's Church), now at the periphery of the square, still stood in a jumble of small streets. The **Neptune fountain** (1891), a work by sculptor Reinhold Begas, originally adorned the forecourt of the royal palace. It is reminiscent of Bernini's *Fountain of the Four Rivers* in Rome, but here the carved figures represent the rivers Elbe, Weichsel, Oder and Rhine.

The **Rotes Rathaus** (Red Town Hall), the red-brick seat of the Mayor of Berlin, is modelled on the buildings of 15th- and 16th-century Italy and Flanders. A frieze of 36 terracotta tablets narrates the history of the city from the 12th century to the founding of the empire in 1871. On 4 November, 1989, a few days before the Wall fell, a demonstration of around 500,000 participants took place on Alexanderplatz.

Passing Time on the Square

In front of the Kaufhaus department store people relax by the **Brunnen der Völkerfreundschaft** (Fountain of the Friendship of Nations), a 1969 work by the sculptor Walter Womacka. You can tell from Erich John's 10m (33-foot) high **Weltzeituhr** (World Time Clock) what time it is anywhere. This is also a favourite meeting-place, perhaps because somewhere in the world it must be the right time to meet. However, no doubt because of the cost, it's apparently not yet time to carry out the grandiose building plans which envisage mighty skyscrapers towering over Alexanderplatz.

Nikolaikirche, Marienkirche and Rotes Rathaus dominate the skyline

Left: Patterns of light below the television tower

TAKING A BREAK

There are lots of snack-bars round the station, and there's also a coffee terrace in the Berlin information bureau at the foot of the television tower.

✚ 193 E3 🚇 Alexanderplatz

Fernsehturm
✉ Panoramastrasse 1a 🏙 Panorama level: daily 9 am–1 am, Mar–Oct; 10 am–midnight, rest of year. Café: daily 10 am–1 am, Mar–Oct; 10–midnight, rest of year 💰 Expensive

ALEXANDERPLATZ: INSIDE INFO

Top tips By the portal of the Marienkirche stands a small white **stone cross**. This expiatory cross was paid for by the repentant Berlin congregation because they had lynched the provost of Bernau in 1324.
• On the banks of the Spree, much to the joy of photographers, are larger-than-life-size **bronze statues** of the philosophers **Marx** and **Engels** (above), created by Ludwig Engelhard in 1986.

Hidden gem On a cloudy or misty day, when you can't see the television tower's globe from below, have a coffee in the café at the top. You'll feel completely removed from the world.

At Your Leisure

4 Kunstwerke Auguststrasse

You walk through the gateway of an old rustic house into a cobbled courtyard. Straight ahead is a slide, and on the left there's a café – but you may be walking through a work of art. Possible, because here the city turns into a small commune with narrow streets. After the fall of the Wall dozens of young artists occupied the dilapidated houses and then, in 1991, four artists moved into a former margarine factory. They founded the Kunst-Werke Berlin (Institute for Contemporary Arts) and began, after makeshift repairs to the building, to organise exhibitions of work by up-and-coming young artists. They are still doing so, but now the building has been renovated, and artists live and work in the wings. In 1998 they organised the *1. berlin biennale für zeitgenössische kunst* (1st berlin biennial for contemporary art – sic), and their exhibitions are always highly praised by international critics.

🚩 192 C3 ✉ Auguststrasse 69 ☎ (030) 243 45 90 🕐 Tue–Sun noon–6 🚇 Oranienburger Tor 🖐 Moderate

For Kids

The largest dinosaur on show anywhere, a 14 million-year-old **Brachiosaurus**, stands 12m (40 feet) high and 23m (75 feet) long in the Museum für Naturkunde (Invalidenstrasse 43, tel: (030) 20 93 85 91, Tue–Fri 9:30–5, Sat–Sun 10–6; U-Bahn station: Zinnowitzer Strasse; admission moderate).

Railway flair in Hamburger Bahnhof exhibition hall

5 Hamburger Bahnhof

Thanks to Dan Flavin, an artist of fluorescent light, a former classical railway station shines out from among the building sites like a blue-green remnant of the Arabian Nights. Especially in the dark, the twinkling green and blue splashes of colour are an irresistible attraction for visitors.

The oldest railway station remaining in the city, Hamburger Bahnhof was in use for exactly 40 years, until replaced by the nearby Lehrter station. It then became a transport museum. In 1996, after the much praised conversion by the architect Josef Paul Kleihues, it became the **Museum für Gegenwart** (Museum of Contemporary Art), an off-shoot of the Neue Nationalgalerie (➤ 108). The breadth and height of the interior are overpowering. It opened with Erich Marx's collection and it now contains some outstanding works: Joseph Beuys' *Tram Stop*, Robert Rauschenberg's *Summer Rental +3*, Andy Warhol's *Mao Portrait*, Cy Twombly's *Sunset Series*, sculptures by Anselm Kiefer and works by Jeff Koons and Matthew Berney. There are also sculptures and drawings by Joseph Beuys and a complete archive of his work.

✚ 192 A4 ✉ Invalidenstrasse 50/51 ☎ (030) 39 78 34 11 🕐 Tue–Fri 10–6, Sat–Sun 11–6, tours Sun 3 pm 🚇 Zinnowitzer Strasse 💳 Moderate; free with *SchauLust* pass (➤ 37)

6 Dorotheenstädtischer Friedhof

The intellectuals and leading lights of Berlin like to be buried in the company of prominent citizens from previous centuries. Karl Friedrich Schinkel, the Prussian architect, is buried in this cemetery, as are the philosophers Johann Fichte and Georg Hegel, the playwright Bertolt Brecht, who founded the Berliner Ensemble theatre, and his wife Helene Weigel. Other Berlin notables buried here include the sculptors Johann Schadow and Christian Rauch, the writers Heinrich Mann, Anna Seghers and Stefan Hermlin, the composers Hanns Eisler and Paul Dessau. Admirers of Heiner Müller, the playwright and director of the Berliner Ensemble, still leave cigars for him in the ashtray on his grave.

✚ 192 B4 ✉ Chausseestrasse 126 🚇 Oranienburger Tor

8 Nikolaiviertel

After World War II, little remained of the historic Nikolaiviertel (St Nicholas Quarter) and until the 1980s there were no buildings opposite Rotes Rathaus except the and the Knoblauchhaus (➤ 88), just grass, pigeons and sparrows. In 1987, as part of Berlin's 750th

A Walk through Spandauer Vorstadt

Dark walls are studded with bullet holes, but much building work is going on; the noise of sawing and the smell of fresh paint are everywhere. Anyone walking through here makes discoveries of sights and points of interest which are not in any guide book, because it's all changing too fast.

Stroll down **Neue Schönhauser Strasse** with its rows of shops, cafés and restaurants. Continue onwards into **Alte Schönhauser Strasse**, turn into Mulackstrasse and try to imagine this as the murky district of underworld bars in the former Barns Quarter (➤ 72).

In **Gormannstrasse** and **Weinmeisterstrasse** you may find yourself fortunate enough to come across exhibitions which no one else has yet seen. Follow interesting looking people into the courtyards, because they may be setting up a gallery or a workplace there. Then you'll begin to understand the absorbing attraction of this area.

A guild emblem in the Nikolaiviertel

jubilee, the area was reconstructed and an "old town" was built, unlike the one that had existed before. Façades crafted from pre-formed concrete slabs were used, together with bow windows and gables, monuments and various other items loaned from other parts of the city, to construct a brand-new historical centre – a perfect socialist Berlin model town. The quarter's most dominant landmark is **Nikolaikirche**, the foundation stones of which are said to have been laid around 1200. The granite blocks of the 13th-century church tower's foundations withstood the war, as did the 14th- to 15th-century stone-work of the choir and nave, but the rest was destroyed. It was rebuilt from 1981 onwards.

Between Poststrasse and the Spree embankment lies the **Ephraimpalais** (Poststrasse 16, open Tue–Sun 10–6, admission moderate or free with *SchauLust* pass ➤ 37), considered by many to be the most beautiful spot in Berlin. It belonged to Veitel Heine Ephraim, court jeweller and banker to Frederick the Great. The appreciative king rewarded him for his loyal service with the gift of columns and balcony railings, booty from the Seven Years War (1756–63). Diagonally opposite is the 18th-century **Knoblauchhaus**; the house was named after the

Volxgolf

Where the Stadion der Weltjugend used to be, there is now a golf centre called Volxgolf, which is very popular with office workers, locals, children and tourists. No plus-fours, no green fees – you just turn up and play, in summer from 7 am onwards, in winter from 8, until the end of your lunch-break or close of business at about 10 pm. You can hire clubs and practice balls for ridiculously little, and you can even have lessons (Chauseestrasse 94–98, tel: (030) 28 04 70 70).

Knoblauch family who owned it until 1928. The 12 rooms, which are part of the Stadtmuseums Berlin (Berlin City Museum), trace the history of both the city and the Knoblauch family (Poststrasse 23, open Tue–Sun 10–6, admission moderate or free with *SchauLust* pass). At Propststrasse 11, a **Zille museum** has been founded, to the memory of the *milieu* painter who recorded the lives of the ordinary citizens of Berlin. There are also old-Berlin (and Italian) eating-houses and good shops for clothes, leather goods and the ubiquitous teddy bears.

🔯 193 E2 ✉ Nikolaiviertel
🚇 Alexanderplatz

Where to...
Eat and Drink

Prices
Prices given are for one person, excluding drinks.
€ under 12 euros €€ 12–25 euros €€€ over 25 euros

RESTAURANTS

Hasir €–€€
The doorman is not there to attract custom, despite appearances. He's there to greet guests, and Turkish hospitality continues when you go in. The staff look after their customers well, it's comfortable inside and pleasant outside. It's hard to know what to choose: lamb dishes or the starter selection? Pitta bread is served with the food; you never go hungry.

🚻 193 D3 ⬛ Oranienburger Strasse 4 ☎ (030) 28 04 16 16 🕐 Daily 11:30–1 am

Le Provençal €€–€€€
The rest of the Nikolaiviertel is dominated by substantial Berlin fare, but here French country dishes are served. Regular guests and francophiles are enticed to the banks of the Spree by rack of lamb, *confit* of goose and, on the French national day (14 July), a delicious *bouillabaisse*.

🚻 193 E2 ⬛ Spreeufer 3 ☎ (030) 302 75 67 🕐 Daily noon–midnight

Maxwell €€–€€€
This is one of Berlin's finest restaurants, attracting artists and their friends. It occupies two storeys and the terrace of a former brewery, which provides a backdrop of neo-Gothic brickwork. Organic products, a cuisine with a modern slant and an extensive wine list guarantee an enjoyable evening.

🚻 192 C3 ⬛ Bergstrasse 22 ☎ (030) 280 71 21 🕐 Daily from 6 pm

Restauration Sophien 11 €
A popular meeting-place, this establishment attracts new Berliners, workers from around the corner and neighbours who want to get together. Try a coffee, a beer and an unpretentious meal in good company.

🚻 193 D3 ⬛ Sophienstrasse 11 ☎ (030) 283 21 36 🕐 Mon–Fri from 5 pm, Sat–Sun from 3 pm

Schwarzenraben €€
In 1890, when the house was built, this was a soup-kitchen for the poor. No longer – it wouldn't fit well into the new designer mile. The high, narrow room is always full, because it's a café in the daytime; the rear part becomes an Italian restaurant in the evening. Later night-owls congregate in the cellar.

🚻 193 E3 ⬛ Neue Schönhauser Strasse 13 ☎ (030) 28 39 16 98 🕐 Café from 10 am, restaurant from 6:30 pm

Zur letzten Instanz €–€€
Opened in 1621 as a brandy saloon, this is probably the oldest inn in the city. Many illustrious guests have sat next to the ancient stove with its majolica tiles: at various times Napoleon and Charlie Chaplin and also the French president Jacques Chirac, who is known to be very fond of good substantial food. On the menu are meatballs with vegetables, goulash and *Eisbein* (knuckle of pork). Some of the names of the dishes derive from legal terms, a reminder of the nearby law courts.

🚻 193 F2 ⬛ Waisenstrasse 14–16 ☎ (030) 242 55 28 🕐 Mon–Sat noon–1 am, Sun noon–11 pm

Where to...
Shop

Most of the shops in Hackesche Höfe don't open until late in the morning. Most of the local customers aren't awake in any case. Here you can find everything hip, or even retro. It's different on Alexanderplatz, which with its station and shops on many levels is the destination of people who work here or are changing trains and in a hurry. The Nikolaiviertel is also a late riser; its shops cater mainly for tourists.

HACKESCHE HÖFE

The courtyards contain some great individual shops. For example, there's **Trippen**, a shoe shop where young people have revived an old tradition, combining workshop and sales. They make trendy wooden shoes, which are also said to be the healthy alternative to conventional footwear.

Several fashion designers display and sell their collections in the courtyards. **Lisa D** has very wearable clothes, but also witty accessories which complement the clothes perfectly; **quasi moda** sells elegant city fashions by four female designers; lovers of the uncomplicated can buy plain, almost minimalist things at **Kostümhaus Jane Garber**.

Hidden away in Hof (Courtyard) V is the **Ampelmännchen-Galerie**, the meaning of which can only be divined by those who know that in Berlin there are two kinds of "Ampelfiguren".

ORANIENBURGER STRASSE

B345un (No 1) has nothing but designer specs as far as the eye can see. **Sterling Gold** (No 32, Heckmann-Höfe) doesn't live up to

Barcomi's Deli

Soak up the atmosphere of this American-style deli where the coffee is roasted and the muffins are baked on the premises. This treasure-house of American food culture also offers bagels, sandwiches and cheesecake.

🚇 193 D3 ⊠ Sophienstrasse 21
☎ (030) 28 59 83 63 ⓒ Mon–Sat 9 am–10 pm, Sun 10–10

Café Bravo

Aubergine (eggplant) for breakfast or breakfast in the evening? Or just the coffee and the art? In this artistic glasshouse everything is possible.

🚇 192 C3 ⊠ Auguststrasse 69
☎ (030) 28 04 49 03 ⓒ Daily 10 am–midnight

Coffeemamas

There's a seductive aroma when you emerge from the S-Bahn station at Hackescher Markt. The ten kinds of coffee are freshly roasted, there are filled bagels, and newspapers to read – but you have to stand.

🚇 193 D3 ⊠ Am Zwinggraben 4
☎ (030) 24 72 22 25 ⓒ Mon–Fri 7 am–8 pm, Sat 10–6, Sun 11–5

Sarah Wieners Speisezimmer

This is not just a café: lunch is also good, according to film crews from around Europe who have been spoilt by the catering service. In any case it's the ideal place for Sunday brunch.

🚇 192 B4 ⊠ Chausseestrasse 8
☎ (030) 69 50 73 37 ⓒ Mon–Fri 9–7, hot meals noon–4.30, breakfast until noon, Sunday brunch 10–5

Zucca

Sparsely but elegantly furnished Zucca, under Hackescher Markt S-Bahn station, reminds you of Italian grand cafés. It's very pleasant sitting in the art deco ambience listening to jazz or pop music.

🚇 193 D3 ⊠ Am Zwingraben
☎ (030) 24 72 12 12 ⓒ Mon–Fri 9 am–3 am, Sat–Sun 10 am–3 am

its name – the shop window contains ball-gowns and cocktail dresses from the 1950s to the 1980s. **Hut up** (No 32) has exciting objects made of felt, from egg-cosies to dresses. **Metamorph** (No 46/47) invites you to disguise yourself with masks of well-known politicians, monsters and various popular celebrities.

ROSENTHALER STRASSE

Everything in the **John de Maya Studio** (No 1) is black and elegant, made of fine materials like cashmere, silk and mohair, in tune with the decor of this designer studio. Six designers have created unconventional clothing, crazy hats and striking jewellery at **Tagebau** (No 19). The 1970s are preserved at **Waahnsinn Berlin**, which has second-hand clothing, nostalgic jewellery and even furniture. Fine pearls and a wide selection of jewellery are displayed in the windows of **Tukadu** (No 46/47).

SOPHIENSTRASSE

Be it a warm woollen plaid, favourite English blends of tea, delicious biscuits, fragrant soap or delicate porcelain, the **British Shop** (No 10) stocks it and sells it. In a minute kitchen, endless varieties of soap are made at **1000 & 1 Seife** (No 28/29). None of the soaps contain industrial additives. At the same address (Paulinenhof) the **Massschuhmacherin** makes shoes to measure to order for both ladies and gentlemen.

ALTE SCHÖNHAUSER STRASSE

At **Lampe:Hinze** (No 6), you'll find a standard collection of lampshades in various styles and colours, made on the premises. The same material is always used: ultra-flexible frosted-polypropylene sheeting.

At **Kochlust** (No 36/37) you can not only get everything for cooking but also arrange to have cookery lessons.

Where to be...
Entertained

Between Rosa-Luxemburg-Platz and Alexanderplatz you won't have to look far if you want to go out at night. The cafés and bars here are open well into the small hours. In the evening a restaurant may become a bar, or later a bar turn into a club. This, as they say, is where it's at.

CULTURE

If you can't decide where to go in the evening, look in one of the city magazines (*tip* or *zitty*). If you trust your judgement, you could always follow those who are already out and about, and who look as though they might have the same tastes as you. With any luck you'll land up in some unlisted place known only to the initiated, whose address and

event timings you'll discover only by chance.

Clubs rarely get going before midnight and if you arrive before then you're likely to find yourself on your own.

In Hackesche Höfe, **Varieté Chamäleon** (tel: (030) 282 71 18) puts on a witty cabaret from Wednesday to Sunday, and also a midnight show on Fridays and Saturdays. The **Hackesche Hoftheater** (tel: (030) 283 25 87) starts its events at variable times. The entrance to **Billardsalon KÖH** (Sophienstrasse 6, Mon–Sat from 5 pm, Sun from 4 pm) is up a flight of steps. The interior is astounding: gold and red, leather sofas, antique furniture, whole shelves of whiskies – an elegant club. You can play pool or cards. You pay by the hour; it's cheaper before 8 pm, and cheaper still on Mondays. Every other Sunday a competition is held – no need to book. The fame of **Kaffee Burger** (Torstrasse 60, tel: (030) 28 04 64 95, daily from 7 pm) has long since spread far beyond Berlin. It has yellow-brown wallpaper and furnishings which even 20 or 30 years ago were old-fashioned. The parties are legendary, especially the Russian disco on the second and fourth Saturday of each month. Thought-provoking readings are held on Sundays: young men – less often women – recite their latest poetic productions, which are criticised mercilessly (though seldom damned out of hand) by the audience.

The **Club der polnischer Versager e. V.** (Torstrasse 66, tel: (030) 28 09 37 79) occasionally invites the public to reading, concerts and film shows. According to its constitution, the club is for "those who are outsiders in their place and time".

At **b-flat** (Rosenthaler Strasse 13, tel: (030) 280 63 49) you can read the jazz programme (Fri–Sun live) in the window, but the club is part of the Swing revival movement as well, so it's also the right place for a dance.

Cox Orange (Dircksenstrasse 40, tel: (030) 281 05 08), a large former apple-cellar, puts on music coming from the East. The **Roten Salon** (on the left) and **Grüner Salon** (Rosa-Luxemburg-Platz 2, on each side of the Volksbühne theatre) hold dances, readings and lectures.

For ten years **Delicious Doughnuts** (Rosenthaler Strasse 9, tel: (030) 28 09 92 74) has been a place to go to in Berlin-Mitte; it's seen dozens of clubs come and go. Pop is the house music in the partly ruined former department store that houses **Tacheles** (Oranienburger Strasse 54–56, tel: (030) 28 09 61 23, ▶ 14). The site is scheduled to be developed, but this venue aims to survive.

BARS

ZeoBar (Rosenthaler Strasse 40/41, tel: (030) 283 46 81, Sun–Thu 5 pm–1 am, Fri–Sat till 2 pm, in summer, daily 7 pm–1 am, in winter) is not a good place to finish off a long evening, because it's right up on the top floor. All the same, the view of the television tower at night is intoxicating.

If you don't want such a climb, stay down in the first courtyard of Hackesche Höfe and go to **Oxymoron** (Rosenthaler Strasse 40/41, tel: (030) 28 39 18 86). In the afternoon it's a romantic coffee-house which, in the evening, then turns into an elegant bar with a retro atmosphere, where you can dance.

A long bar counter, yellow and dark brown benches, and people standing at the bar or outside the door with a drink are characteristic of **fc magnet** (Veteranenstrasse 26, tel: (030) 48 49 50 49). No one dresses up here. The music is rather dark and electronic – just what

you'd expect from a night-club. The real centres of attraction for Berliners, though, are the well-known footballers who frequent this establishment.

In every respect, **Kurvenstar** (Kleine Präsidentenstrasse 3, tel: (030) 28 59 97 10, daily from 8 pm) is a mixture of styles borrowed from the 1960s and 1970s. Decide for yourself whether it's a bar, a dive, a restaurant or a club, and whether the whole thing is kitschy or cool.

The colourful **Riva** bar in the S-Bahn arches (Dircksenstrasse, arch 142, tel: (030) 24 72 26 88, daily from 6 pm) is named after the Sardinian football star Luigi Riva. The customers are chic and the cocktails are classic.

Connoisseurs find their way to the Russian library in the **Tarakan Bar** (Linienstrasse 154a, tel: (030) 28 09 49 92, daily from 8 pm) where Russian caviar is served in little bowls amid red walls and golden ornaments.

Potsdamer Platz

Getting Your Bearings

The foundation stone for 21st-century Berlin was laid in 1994, since when millions of people from across the world have come to see the new city growing from nothing on Europe's biggest building site. Now it's almost finished, and you can assess how well it works.

Before the war there were department stores and cabarets on Potsdamer Platz – it was one of Europe's noisiest and most exciting squares. And because the traffic police at the centre couldn't make themselves heard, in 1925 they had to install the first traffic lights, imported from New York. Barely 70 years later, the bleak Potsdamer Platz has suddenly become a visionary place, where dreams are expressed in stone and glass.

Across the way, on the Kulturforum, the Philharmonic (▶ 107) shines golden. It's on the edge of an area which was for decades the last outpost of the West, and so it became the site of artistic centres.

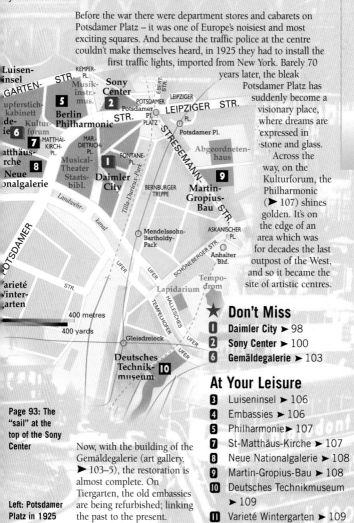

Page 93: The "sail" at the top of the Sony Center

Left: Potsdamer Platz in 1925

Now, with the building of the Gemäldegalerie (art gallery, ▶ 103–5), the restoration is almost complete. On Tiergarten, the old embassies are being refurbished; linking the past to the present.

★ Don't Miss

At Your Leisure

It's all new. It's hard to imagine that until a few years ago this was just rough ground bordering the Wall which separated East from West.

Potsdamer Platz in a Day

10:00 am
Start the day in ❶ **Daimler City's** (➤ 98–9) Alter Potsdamer Strasse with breakfast in a café (above). The trees are already tall enough to provide shade.

11:00 am
Stroll through the narrow streets and judge for yourself whether the internationally renowned architects' grand plans are a success. Go into the basilica-like DaimlerChrysler Services building, opposite the Musical-Theater on Marlene-Dietrich-Platz, and have a look at the art on display in the public areas. DaimlerChrysler Contemporary in Weinhaus Huth (➤ 99) is also worth a visit. If you like, book tickets for a show in the Imax cinema (left; ➤ 99). Take the lift up to the viewing terrace of the Kollhoff skyscraper (➤ 99); the whole of Berlin lies at your feet.

12:00 noon

Crossing Potsdamer Strasse, you come to the **2 Sony Center** (➤ 100–102); pause by the fountain and soak up the atmosphere. All around is one of the high points of the capital's architecture. Prepare to be amazed by the presentation in the Filmmuseum (➤ 101).

1:00 pm

The Café Josty in the neo-rococo breakfast room of the 1908 Grandhotel Esplanade (➤ 100–1) is just right for a lunch-break. If you need to get away from stone and glass for a while, cross Kemperplatz on the other side of the Entlastungsstrasse (relief road) and follow the path to **3 Luiseninsel** (Luise Island; ➤ 106) across Tiergarten. Children can play here, and adults can stretch out on the grass.

3:00 pm

Follow Tiergartenstrasse past the **4 Embassies** (➤ 106) till you get to the **5 Berlin Philharmonic** (above; ➤ 107), home of the Berlin Philharmonic orchestra, on the Kulturforum. Take time out for a visit to the **6 Gemäldegalerie** (➤ 103–5). Or there might be an interesting exhibition at the **8 Neue Nationalgalerie** (New National Gallery) (➤ 108) or the **9 Martin-Gropius-Bau** (➤ 108). If the children grumble, take them to the **10 Deutsches Technikmuseum** (German Museum of Technology) (➤ 109) instead.

6:00 pm

Look for a place for dinner, perhaps at Potsdamer Platz 1 (➤ 110), and then spoil yourself with a visit to **11 Varieté Wintergarten** (left; ➤ 109).

Daimler City

You won't find Daimler City on any plan of Berlin; it's just one half of Potsdamer Platz, standing in unmistakable contrast to the Sony Center opposite.

Renzo Piano collaborated with the British architect Richard Rogers to create the overall concept for the area, when reconstruction began in the early 1990s. The design brief was to fill a site of some 7ha (17 acres) with 19 separate buildings, creating the centre of a metropolis. It was to be full of life, day and night, with flats, offices, businesses and places of entertainment. Fourteen architects' practices from across the globe were invited to submit and the buildings were designed in Tokyo, London, Munich, Milan, Madrid and Berlin.

You are welcomed on Potsdamer Strasse by Keith Haring's colourful **Boxers**. With its warm terracotta façade, the headquarters of **DaimlerChrysler Services** stretch up to the sky like a cathedral. The ventilation stack from the Tiergarten tunnel can be seen for miles, crowned with the firm's logo, an emerald-green cube. At the entrance you are met by one of the works of art commissioned for the building's public areas, Korean Nam June Paik's flickering video and neon-tube installation. In the seven-storey atrium, beams of blue light, an installation by François Morellet, lead your eyes upwards. Down below you hear the continual rattle and squeak of the wheels of Jean Tinguelys' sculpture **Méta Maxi**, reminding us that time never stands still.

Left: The headquarters of DaimlerChrysler Services

The heavy mob: Haring's Boxers

Right: Jeff Koons's flower sculpture

A City Gathers Pace

The foundation stone was laid in October 1994. In the 1996 topping-out ceremony, Daniel Barenboim conducted, not a famous orchestra, but swaying building cranes. Potsdamer Platz was officially opened in 1998.

3-D Cinema

Casino and music-hall meet in the shell-shaped, tiered **Marlene-Dietrich-Platz**, with its descending streams of water. Passers-by are reflected in Jeff Koons's sculpture, a blue flower of tethered balloons. From close by you can hardly see the bright blue dome above the **Imax cinema**, known to detractors as the "giants' school telly". A screen as high as a seven-storey house projects 3-D images at the spectators, which plunge them into submarine worlds or transport them into the desert.

The Fastest Lift on the Continent

The refurbished **Weinhaus Huth**, the only old house left standing here, now houses DaimlerChrysler Contemporary, an exhibition of 20th-century art. The 5-star Hyatt Hotel has a fitness centre on the roof, concealing a swimming-pool and panoramic view accessible only to members of the appropriately expensive club. One can at least look down from the pointed, brick-red high-rise **Kollhof building** with golden pinnacles, which the Berlin architect Hans Kollhoff designed on the model of New York skyscrapers. The fastest lift on the continent carries its passengers to the 24th floor extremely smoothly in 20 seconds. From here, you might almost think you could step into the offices of Deutsche Bank in the **Sony Center** (➤ 100–1) on the opposite side of the square, or land with a short leap in Tiergarten.

TAKING A BREAK

Salomon Bagels on the upper floor of the Potsdamer Platz arcades will come to the aid of hungry and thirsty visitors.

➕ 196 A3/4 ✉ Potsdamer Platz ⊚ Potsdamer Platz

Imax Cinema

✉ Marlene-Dietrich-Platz 4 ☎ Recorded programme information (030) 25 92 72 59, reservations 01805 / 46 29 22 55 (about 0.12 € per minute) ⏰ Advance bookings daily 10–10

Viewing Platform

✉ Potsdamer Strasse 1 ⏰ Daily 11–8 ✋ Expensive

2 Sony Center

High above the Plaza the "big top" catches the light, bouncing
it off reflecting glass in waves of violet, blue and sunset red.
Down below the Grandhotel Esplanade, transported in space
and time, is displayed behind transparent walls.

The completed Daimler City was received by Berliners with a
non-commital "Ye-e-s" and a shrug of the shoulders, but when
they saw the finished Sony Center in June 2000 they let out an
enthusiastic "Zowie!". A small, but quite new kind of city had
come into being. Nothing but glass and steel, which you are
hardly aware of, but everything reflects everything else,
creating an illusion of distance and multiplicity.

**Right: A room
in the
Grandhotel
Esplanade**

Colourful Tent

The 130m (425-foot) high **glass half-globe** on the Potsdamer
Platz frontage earned the architect Helmut Jahn the nickname of
"*Turmvater* (tower-father) *Jahn*". The most amazing part of Jahn's
design, though, is the tent-roof, supported by steel hawsers and
rods, covering the courtyard at the heart of the complex. In the
changing evening light, now light blue, now violet, it engenders
a magical vitality. In the plaza below, a fountain splashes away
quietly, waking up now and then to send bright jets of water
into the night. Up in the tent the wind rustles and ruffles the
material, then suddenly sweeps down through the glass ravines
and gives the site its own repertoire of sounds.

**The protective
tent roof over
the plaza**

Floating on Air into the Future

After the fall of the Wall, when Sony bought the site, the old
Grandhotel Esplanade stood on the edge of it. The 1908 de

uxe hotel was badly damaged in World War II and the large reception rooms were used only for occasional films and carnival dances. The house stood in the way of the proposed development, but the city authorities were anxious

The Kaiser's WC
The lavatory under the Kaisersaal has been restored to its original state, with brass door handles, wooden seats and marble urinals from the late 19th century. The Kaiser himself once washed his hands in these wash-basins.

that it should be preserved. So began an architectural venture which cost 50 million Marks. The Rote Salon (Red Salon), in which Kaiser Wilhelm II held his gentlemen's evenings, was scooped out of the Esplanade, and transported 75m (80 yards) on air cushions, so that it could be incorporated into the new building. The whole job took 20 days, with the supervisors always worried that it wouldn't work; after all, it was a first for all concerned.

Apartments Suspended over the Palm Court

The Palmenhof (Palm Court) and Silbersaal (Silver Hall) remained where they were, but the neo-rococo breakfast room had to be moved. Two of the room's walls were cut into 500 pieces and re-assembled in a glass casing. Two internal walls are now external walls, behind glass. In order not to overload the old building, the architect suspended six storeys of apartments from a bridging construction. These apartments are now among the most expensive in Berlin.

Just Like the Movies

The Sony Centre's next visual pleasure awaits you in half-light as you take the lift up to the **Filmmuseum**: almost other-worldly will-o'-the wisps of light flash around the courtyard. You enter the film museum – and are completely absorbed. It takes time to get used to the intensity of the light and the reflections from the mirrors. Then wander through the history of the German cinema. The separate section on artificial worlds traces the history of fantasy and sci-fi films.

For Kids
Children vanish in the Sony Center as soon as they catch sight of the **Sony Style Store**, which promises electronic pleasures of every kind: MP3 players, spectacles with built-in video, high-tech systems – and it's all hands-on, even for tomorrow's customers.

The Berlinale
The real film world is here every February. Since the 50th Berlinale international film festival in 2000, the red carpets have been rolled out on Potsdamer Platz for the benefit of film stars from across the globe, who are

Sky Above Berlin

On Potsdamer Platz, 14 years before the Berlin film festival was first held there in 2000, Wim Wenders shot his film *Der Himmel über Berlin* (*Wings of Desire*). He got 86-year-old Curt Bois to run, quite alone, round a completely deserted and desolate square repeating again and again: "*Ich kann den Potsdamer Platz nicht finden...*" ("I can't find Potsdamer Platz...").

cheered by Berliners and visitors alike, until echoes ring around the plaza. The Musical-Theater (➤ 112) opposite Daimler City is temporarily turned into a cinema and the whole square becomes a show-case for the film world – and Berlin.

TAKING A BREAK

Billy Wilder's (Potsdamer Strasse 2) is a pleasant place for a coffee, cakes or snacks. The exotic drinks and cocktails are also worth a try.

Like two peas in a pod: cinema and reality

➕ 196 A4 ✉ Potsdamer Platz 🚇 Potsdamer Platz

Filmmuseum
☎ (030) 300 90 30 🕐 Tue–Sun 10–6, Thu 10–8 💶 Moderate

Left: The Berlinale bear

SONY CENTER: INSIDE INFO

Top tip The **CineStar** cinema (Potsdamer Strasse 4, tel: (030) 26 06 62 60) shows almost all films in the original language, with subtitles in German.

Hidden gems The Filmmuseum also owns the **Arsenal** art film cinema (Potsdamer Strasse 2, tel: (030) 26 95 51 00) which, for more than 30 years, has documented the history and culture of the cinema across the world; it puts on a succession of special programmes.
• Down in the **U-Bahn station** there are sometimes interesting installations or other works of art to see or hear.
• Volkswagen-sponsored **ZOON.COM** is an innovative area where kids can explore all facets of the internet (free).

⑥ Gemäldegalerie

In 1998 East and West Berlin's stocks of paintings were brought together in the Kulturforum to form one of the most valuable collections in the world. In numerous halls and display cases 1,000 examples of Western painting are on show. Another 500 hang in the rooms of the Studiengalerie (study gallery).

He Who Digs a Pit For Others...

A fascinating picture hangs in room 7, **Flemish Proverbs**, painted in 1559 by Pieter Bruegel the Elder. In it a whole village is on the move, and you can spend absorbing minutes trying to work out the proverbs depicted. What's the man, bottom left, by the wall doing? Is he trying to shove his head through it? Diagonally above him someone is worried about unlaid eggs. In the centre foreground a person is casting roses (or are they pearls?) before swine, and in front of him another is digging a pit. The picture illustrates exactly 100 sayings and proverbs, four and a half centuries old but timeless.

The entrance hall is a surprise: not a single picture is to be seen, only a sculpture, Walter de Maria's **5-7-9 Series**. The special quality of the place becomes evident as you go round. Pillars and projecting walls divide the space into 33 areas, and through a round window above each you can see the sky, evocative of the Roman Pantheon, but that is the only dramatic touch in an otherwise unspectacular building. Admittedly, though, the Munich architects' firm Hilmer & Sattler did succeed in pulling off the trick of creating a gallery lit by daylight but without shadows.

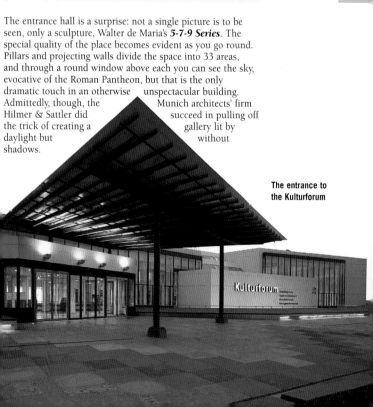

The entrance to the Kulturforum

Gallery Highlights

It's impossible to see everything in a single day so, to help you choose, here are some of the highlights. You can wander through the history of painting, starting in Saal (hall) I with the **Enthroned Virgin with Child** (c1340), which shows how at that time, when few could read, it was size which indicated a person's importance. And while in the Middle Ages painters took their topics from biblical stories and saints, later these gave way to commissioned works like Albrecht Dürer's **Hieronymus Holzschuh** (1526) in Raum (room) 2. Every hair is distinct in the furs worn by a man wealthy enough to afford such a portrait. With Titian's **Venus with Organ Player** (c1550, Saal XV) the concept of the picture derives from the philosophy of antiquity: three kinds of beauty are to be seen, spiritual, physical and musical.

In Thomas Gainsborough's painting **The Marsham Children** (1787, Raum 20) man and nature are reconciled. It seems almost expressionistic in style, but in fact the Romantic painter and celebrated portraitist to aristocrats and the upper middle class was influenced in his late work by the French painter Watteau.

A Tour of the Gallery

This tour takes you round the halls and rooms of the gallery in an anticlockwise (counterclockwise) direction. Starting at Saal (hall) I, on the right of the entrance, halls I to III feature the old German masters (13th–16th centuries). The route continues via the early Dutch painters (15th–16th centuries; IV–VI), the 17th-century Flemish and Dutch paintings (VII–XI), works from Britain, France and Germany (18th century; 20–22) to halls XII to XIV with paintings from Italy (17th–18th centuries), France (17th century) and Spain (16th–17th centuries). Finally, it arrives at the 15th–16th-century Italians (XV–XVII), miniaturists (34) and the 13th–15th-century Italians (XVIII). The study gallery is on the lower ground floor, and the digital gallery is in rooms 27, 33 and 42. It's advisable to pick up a plan of the gallery at the entrance.

Titian's *Venus with Organ Player* (detail)

Thomas Gainsborough's *The Marsham Children*

Other great paintings held by the gallery include works by Hans Holbein, Van Eyck, Rembrandt and Raphael.

TAKING A BREAK

There's a café at the entrance, but in fine weather you may prefer to sit by the snack-bar on the forecourt.

✚ 195 F4 ✉ Matthäikirchplatz 8 ☎ (030) 266 29 51 🕐 Tue–Wed, Fri–Sun 10–6, Thu 10–10 🚇 Potsdamer Platz 💷 Moderate

---

GEMÄLDEGALERIE: INSIDE INFO

Top tips On the **first Sunday of the month** all the museums of the Kulturforum are free (Musikinstrumentenmuseum (musical instruments), Kupferstichkabinett (engravings), Kunstgewerbemuseum (arts and crafts), Neue Nationalgalerie ➤ 108). All museums are also covered by the *SchauLust* pass (➤ 37).

• The three-day **Museumspass** gives entry to about 50 museums. If you visit more than two museums, it works out cheaper.

• **Thematic tours** (topics such as the Old Testament, Strong Women in Painting, etc.) are held on Tuesdays at 11 am, Saturdays at 11 am and 2:30 pm, and Sundays at 2:30 pm.

• There are **guided tours for children** on Sundays at 2:30 pm.

• The "Kunst macht mobil" ("Art gets you moving") event is held every Wednesday at 11 am for **wheelchair users** (booking essential).

At Your Leisure

3 Luiseninsel

On the other side of Tiergartenstrasse from the Philharmonie and the Kulturforum is the Tiergarten, the largest green space in the inner city. Long views – for example to the Grosser Stern with the Siegessäule column – help with orientation. To the southwest of Bellevue-Allee a path leads to Luiseninsel (Luise Island), on the southern edge of Tiergarten. This part of the park was laid out in the 19th century by the royal director of the Tiergarten Eduard Neide, with a statue of Prussia's popular queen Luise at its centre. On the 750th anniversary of the city, the princely environment was restored when flower-beds were replanted. Luise had not seen her husband Friedrich Wilhelm III for a long time, till the thicket which had grown up between the two statues was removed.

➕ 195 F4 🚇 Potsdamer Platz

4 Embassies

It takes only five minutes to walk from Japan to Egypt, or rather from Hiroshimastrasse via Tiergartenstrasse to Stauffenbergstrasse. The southern side of Tiergartenstrasse is the diplomatic quarter. Before World War II embassies stood shoulder to shoulder here; many have returned but there are still gaps, because not every country has the funds for a suitably lavish building. It's clear, though, that some have spared no expense. The **Japanese embassy** on the corner of Hiroshimastrasse and Tiergartenstrasse has been rebuilt on a colossal scale. The original house, built in 1942 but badly damaged in the war, was demolished in the 1980s. Now it has been replaced by a 14,000sq m (16,750 square yard) embassy, residence and cultural centre. Opposite it, in **Greek** territory, rampant vegetation covers a ruin where birch trees have taken root. On Tiergartenstrasse, **Italy** has presented its ambassador with a veritable palace: flights of steps, columns and doors from a historic Doge's palace adorn the red-rendered house. **Estonia** has been content with a renovated late 19th-century villa. **Turkey** is biding its time. **South Africa** intends to reflect African

culture and tradition in its architectural style, for example with extensive roof terraces. The red stone for the **Indian** embassy was shipped from Rajastan to Berlin. "Only truth prevails", says the inscription on the national coat of arms by the entrance. On the corner of Stauffenbergstrasse, **Austria** presents itself in glittering green copper. **Egypt** hides behind severe geometrical forms.

🔲 195 F4 ☒ Hiroshimastrasse, Tiergartenstrasse, Stauffenbergstrasse
🚇 Potsdamer Platz

🖪 Berlin Philharmonic

The exterior of Hans Scharoun's building (1960–3), with its undulating silhouette and golden façade, is already enough to draw the eye, but the interior provides the real experience. Even those who don't go much to symphony concerts may still see something in the programme of events which they can enjoy. Besides the Berlin Philharmonic orchestra, many guest orchestras, chamber music groups and soloists perform

here. Juliette Greco has sung here, and so has Hildegard Knef. But connoisseurs enthuse about the sound of the Berlin Philharmonic, and since Sir Simon Rattle has been their resident conductor they have not ceased to sing its praises: an orchestra which can also be the greatest quartet in the world, if the music demands it. In the centre of the building stands the orchestra platform, around which the architect has ranged terraced seating for an audience of 2,200. The effect is informal and yet serious, and the acoustics under the suspended sound-boards are marvellous.

🔲 196 A4 ☒ Herbert-von-Karajan-Strasse 1 ☎ (030) 25 48 81 32
🕐 Box office Mon–Fri 3–6, Sat–Sun 11–2 🚇 Potsdamer Platz

🖪 St-Matthäus-Kirche

Surrounded as it is by new building, the little church which gives the square its name looks as if it has emerged from the wrong box of bricks. Designed in the 19th century by classical architect Karl Friedrich Schinkel's pupil Friedrich August Stüler, it was due to be demolished in the 20th century, along with all the surrounding houses. Hitler's architect Albert Speer had plans for a "world capital – Germania", and this district didn't fit in with them. Things turned out differently, the church was damaged in the war and rebuilt in 1959–60. The pulpit, much praised for its acoustics, has regained its gabled canopy. Groups of slender windows break up the long, brick-built side walls. On the gallery wall in front of the organ hangs *Antlitz (Face)*, a sculpture by Vadim Sidur, one of the most important sculptors of

Around Potsdamer Platz: like a page from an architectural picture book

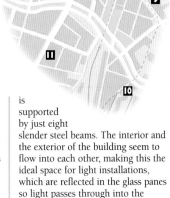

the Moscow alternative art scene. Out of a dented bucket Sidur has created an object with a face on both sides.

Exhibitions, concerts and theatrical performances are regularly staged in the church.

➕ 195 F4 ✉ Matthäikirchplatz
🕐 Tue–Sun noon–6; Tue–Sat 12:30–12:50 worship accompanied by organ music 🚇 Potsdamer Platz
💷 Free

🎱 Neue Nationalgalerie

The secret of the New National Gallery's attraction for all visitors to the Kulturforum is no doubt the fact that you can see right into the building from outside, whereas all its neighbours hide their inner life behind stone. This unique museum was built in 1968 by the architect Mies van der Rohe, a commission which drew him back to Berlin after he had emigrated to the USA. His glass and steel temple is a contemporary interpretation of the Alte Nationalgalerie on Museumsinsel (► 78–9). He is said to have called his design "*die Halle an sich*" ("The hall-in-itself"). The saddle-roof

Display tablet on the façade of the Gropius building

is supported by just eight slender steel beams. The interior and the exterior of the building seem to flow into each other, making this the ideal space for light installations, which are reflected in the glass panes so light passes through into the darkness outside. Among the high points of the pictures and sculptures exhibited on the lower-ground floor are the works of the critical realists of the 1920s, George Grosz (1893–1959) and Otto Dix (1891–1969).

➕ 195 F4 ✉ Potsdamer Strasse 50
☎ (030) 266 26 62 🕐 Tue, Wed, Fri 10–6, Thu 10–10, Sat–Sun 11–6
🚇 Potsdamer Platz 💷 Moderate; free with *SchauLust* pass (► 37)

🎵 Martin-Gropius-Bau

This is a house that looks like an exhibition, as it was intended to. The building, which bears the architect's name, was constructed in 1877–81 as a museum where students at the arts and crafts school could study the exhibits. Reliefs and mosaics made the façade into a display of artistic handiwork. Until the 1970s the war-damaged building was threatened with demolition, because it stood in the way of a proposed urban motorway. In 1977–81 it was restored and now counts as Berlin's finest exhibition building. In 1999 it was renovated to be able to host large prestigious exhibitions.

➕ 196 B3 ✉ Niederkirchner Strasse 7 ☎ (030) 25 48 60 🕐 Wed–Mon 10–8 🚇 Anhalter Bahnhof

The last landing of a *Rosinenbomber*

⑩ Deutsches Technikmuseum

The C47 Skytrain, which was a *Rosinenbomber* ("raisin bomber", ➤ 12) bringing supplies to West Berlin during the 1948–9 air lift, seems to be about to land on Potsdamer Platz, but in fact its last landing place is on the roof of the Deutsches Technikmuseum. That fits well with the museum, where old steam-engines thud and wooden hand-presses print characters onto paper. Another part of the technological history of humankind is the television studio of 1958, the only recording room of the period still functioning – in black and white. In 1963, when it was first used in Berlin, the camera captured John F Kennedy's unforgettable words. *"Ich bin ein Berliner"* ("I am a Berliner").

You can inspect a historic brewery, vintage cars and trains, but the most fascinating part for many – especially children and young people – is **Spectrum**, a hands-on area in which visitors can carry out their own scientific experiments.

➕ 196 B2 ✉ Trebbiner Strasse 9, Spectrum Science Center Möckernstrasse 26/Anhalter Güterbahnhof ☎ (030) 90 25 40

🕓 Tue–Fri 9–5, Sat–Sun 10–6
Ⓜ Gleisdreieck, Möckernbrücke
💶 Moderate; free with *SchauLust* pass (➤ 37)

⑪ Varieté Wintergarten

At the top of a red carpet a uniformed gentleman opens the door for you. You enter a space furnished with fine warm mahogany, polished brass and red plush velvet, under a canopy spangled with thousands of little twinkling lights. The side walls are decorated with ceiling-high showcases filled with valuable props and costumes used by legendary variety artistes. But all this simply provides the atmosphere which complements and creates a backdrop for the main attraction – the variety shows. Great variety artistes and internationally known magicians help you to forget the world for a few hours. Bernhard Paul (director and founder of Circus Roncalli) with his friend and colleague André Heller founded the venture in 1992, and its success has proved them right.

➕ 195 F3 ✉ Potsdamer Strasse 96
☎ (030) 25 00 88 88 🕓 Box Office
Mon–Fri 10–6, Sat 10–4, Sun 2–6
Ⓜ Kurfürstenstrasse

Where to...
Eat and Drink

Prices

Prices given are for one person, excluding drinks.
€ under 12 euros **€€** 12–25 euros **€€€** over 25 euros

RESTAURANTS

Dietrich's Bistro €

This large bar has high tables with stools. The enormous turkey, bacon and fried egg sandwiches are highly recommended. There are also salads for vegetarians, in addition to bagels, burgers and a daily Italian dish.

➕ 196 A4 ☒ Marlene-Dietrich-Platz 2 ☎ (030) 25 53 17 88 ⏱ Mon–Fri 11 am–1 am, Sat–Sun 10 am–2 am

Einstein €€

Sample the epitome of Viennese style in the former villa of the German actor Henny Porten. This is truly a classic coffee-house, a must for intellectuals of the café society who also know the difference between *Melange* (Mix) and *Kleines Braunes* (Small Brown). But be warned: if you don't, you may be exposed to the disapproving glances of waiters in their smart aprons. The floors are of marble, the chair seats of satin. Of course the tables are really too small to get to work on a *Wiener schnitzel*, but for the excellent *Sachertorte* (rich chocolate cake) they are just right. The beautiful garden is particularly suitable for relaxing with a newspaper. Really stylish!

➕ 195 E3 ☒ Kurfürstenstrasse 58 ☎ (030) 261 50 96 ⏱ Daily 9 am–2 am; dish of the day noon–3 pm

Joseph Roth Diele €

No more than two dishes of the day, a soup and a simple menu are served here, written up on a board behind the bar counter. In other ways, too, this inn is different from the usual German inn. Wooden benches, divans from Morocco, light alcoves – ideal as reading corners. Long ago the house was a confectioner's. When the then owners were clearing out what had been a warehouse they found a fine stone floor and old recipes for pastries. And they discovered that in the 1920s the Austrian writer Joseph Roth lived next door and had begun to write a novel in the café. The sausages and stews are supplied by a Franciscan house in Brandenburg, and a small picture of a saint is a modest reference to its neighbour, the religious shop Ave Maria (▶ 111).

➕ 195 F3 ☒ Potsdamer Strasse 75 ☎ (030) 26 36 98 84 ⏱ Mon–Fri 10–10; lunch menu noon–3 pm

Potsdamer Platz 1 €-€€

Preferred by leisurely eaters, this restaurant serves a modified German cuisine. Depending on the time of year, there's marinaded pumpkin and *Königsberger Klopse* (meatballs), roasts and swede (turnip).

➕ 196 A4 ☒ Potsdamer Platz 1 ☎ (030) 25 37 89 45 ⏱ Daily 11 am–1 am

Tizian €€-€€€

This elegant Italian restaurant in the Hyatt Hotel is one of the best, if not *the* best, on Potsdamer Platz. The cooking is excellent and the decor cool and uncluttered. From the hors-d'oeuvres to the *tiramisu*, you really can't go wrong.

➕ 196 A4 ☒ Marlene-Dietrich-Platz 2 ☎ (030) 25 53 17 64 ⏱ Daily 8 am–midnight

Where to... Shop

POTSDAMER STRASSE

Potsdamer Strasse runs over the Landwehrkanal down to Schöneberg, a bleak street with grey houses, which is only gradually being brightened up by Turkish businesses and junk shops. All the same, the Varieté Wintergarten (▶ 109) and, on the other side of the road, the publishing house of the newspaper *Tagesspiegel* indicate a growing sophistication.

Next door to the *Tagesspiegel* is a small shop which merits attention. **Ave Maria** (Potsdamer Strasse 75, Mon–Fri noon–7, Sat noon–3) has a tinge of Lourdes, in France, about it. Not only does it stock countless types of incense, there are also Madonnas with flashing eyes, and crucifixes, in sizes suitable for the

car or the handbag, shining out in pseudo-baroque splendour. Anyone looking for a votive offering will find a selection of silver arms and legs, which pilgrims offer in the hope of being cured of every sort of ill. And there are candles, big and small, consecrated or not.

POTSDAMER PLATZ ARCADES

Things are more conventional in the Potsdamer Platz Arcades. The **lower ground floor** has the services, like passport photos to ATMs (cash machines), as well as drugstores and pharmacies, pizza and fish snack-bars, coffee shops and groceries, with branches of well-known clothing chains. On the **ground floor**, lovers of fine (and expensive) leather goods will find what they seek at Bree. Hallhuber, Eddie Bauer, Mango and Mexx stock fashionable clothing. Swarovski has fine crystal. Brando 4 and Modebewusste are on the **upper floor**, where Swatch Store has a vast selection of colourful watches.

Where to be... Entertained

People with tickets for the Philharmonic (▶ 107) or for Varieté Wintergarten (▶ 109) have nothing to worry about. If you want to dance or go out for a drink in this area, there's not much to choose from. Then, if not before, you'll realise that Potsdamer Platz **is still not a fully developed district.**

NIGHT-CLUBS

"Beauty, Glam and Fame" is the motto of **Dorian Gray** (Marlene-Dietrich-Platz 4, tel: (030) 25 93 06 60; Tue After Work Party, Thu Gay-Disko, Fri 27'up, Sat all welcome). This temple of dance is intended to be a reminder of one of Germany's most unusual discos, held in the cellars of Frankfurt airport. Its

famous Saturday-Night-Fever-Time dates admittedly from 1978, when the international jet-set met there. In the 1980s the DJ Talla 2XLC saw to it that dancing to Techno music went on all night. On 1 January, 2001, stricter fire safety regulations meant that the Frankfurt dance-floor had to close, so in spring 2003 its originators came to the capital.

CINEMAS

Every day visitors to Potsdamer Platz have the choice over almost two dozen films in the **Multiplex cinemas** in Daimler City (Potsdamer Platz 1–19) and the Sony Center (Potsdamer Strasse 4). Some are shown in the original language with German subtitles, and there are special treats for film buffs at **Arsenal** (▶ 102). The **Imax cinema** (▶ 99) offers a quite new film experience. The name of this sumptuous film theatre means Image Maximization, that is, enlargement of the picture to its maximum. The gigantic screen of 1,000sq m (nearly 1,200 square yards) hanging under a dome draws the audience right into the action. Fragments of a volcanic eruption appear to fly past your head, with the lava flowing at your feet. There is seating for 440 spectators arranged in 13 rows, one behind the other at a steep angle of 33 degrees. Virtually nothing but films about the natural world are shown. This type of cinema already exists in more than 20 countries.

THEATRE

The **Musical-Theater**, a traditional two-level theatre (Marlene-Dietrich-Platz 1, tel: 01805/11 41 13) holds 1,800 spectators. Though nobody really knows why, Berlin has never

had a good experience with musicals. Their runs are shorter than in other cities, perhaps because the choice of entertainment is more varied than elsewhere. During the Berlinale film festival the theatre becomes a cinema.

CASINOS

Holiday money all gone? The casino under the Musical-Theater (Marlene-Dietrich-Platz 1, tel: (030) 25 59 90) offers the chance to win it back at roulette, baccarat and black-jack. In addition, rows of one-armed bandits and other machines await the gambler. The slot-machine room downstairs (daily 10:30 am–2:30 am) is already full of smoke in the morning. The "beautiful people" come later to the casino (no tie required 2 pm–midnight), and the select few play in the evening (when the public is excluded, so to speak) in the Casino Royal (8 pm–3 am, tie essential!).

BARS

The word has got around: *Caroshi* is Japanese for "death by overwork". The **Caroshi Bar** (Linkstrasse 4, tel: (030) 25 29 33 52, daily 11 am–2 am) prevents this firstly with *sushi*, then with brightly coloured cocktails. Very relaxing

The **Kara-Kas Bar** (Kurfürstenstrasse 9, tel: (030) 265 21 71, Tue–Thu and Sat 9 pm–2 am, Fri–Sat 9 pm–5 am), the oldest Latino bar in the west of Berlin, has roses on the ceiling and Latin-American rhythms down below. Its concerts and exhibitions don't only attract the regulars.

Anyone who's never been to **Kumpelnest 3000** (Lützowstrasse 23, tel: (030) 261 69 18, daily from 5 pm) knows nothing about Berlin's night-life. Next day, those who stay too long will wonder during which film they lost count of time. Kumpelnest sweeps up office parties, people leaving private functions, the insatiable from bars

which close earlier, those curious to know who's still about... It's an address where no one is too old if they still like listening to Abba or don't particularly care what the music is.

In **Puschel's Pub** (Potsdamer Strasse 112, tel: 0175/ 854 73 34, daily from 3 pm) young Schönebergers make friends with people staying at the nearby youth hostel. The landlord is a fan of German soccer team Bayern Munich and likes watching televised soccer in company.

The **Vox Bar** in the Grand Hyatt (Marlene-Dietrich-Platz 2, tel: (030) 25 53 12 34, daily from 6 pm, live music from 10 pm) is decked out in black and red. The Martinis are dry, and served with a piece of ginger instead of the usual olive. Some customers may prefer to choose from the 200 kinds of whisky, for which the bar is renowned. The music features the greats of jazz and soul, which ensures a tremendous night-club atmosphere.

Around the Kurfürstendamm

Getting Your Bearings

Schloss
Charlottenburg
4

SPANDAUER DAMM
LUISENPL.
7 **6** Ägyptische
Museum
Sammlung
Berggruen
SCHLOSS-
STR.
KAISER-FRIEDRICH-STR.
R.—W

"Ich hab' so Heimweh nach dem Kurfürstendamm" (I'm so homesick for Kurfürstendamm). This one song line was enough for West Berliners to take the singer Hildegard Knef to their hearts. After the partitioning of the city in 1961, Kudamm, as it's known here, became their new centre. It had always been Berlin's equivalent of the Champs-Élysées in Paris, and it has remained the favourite shopping, promenading and people-watching street.

After the fall of the Wall hardly anyone mentioned Kudamm. "Berlin" meant Unter den Linden, Spandauer Vorstadt or Potsdamer Platz. It seemed that no one was interested in the west of the city. Now people drive there again, stroll down the avenue and into the side streets, and enjoy their special atmosphere.

Kurfürstendamm has an adult charm; the streets in which people live, go about their daily business and enjoy their leisure time are lively and boisterous. Any new addition soon fits in with whatever was already there. Well, usually.

Schloss Charlottenburg and its parks provide oases, used as much by locals as by visitors.

The heart of Berlin beats in Breitscheidplatz. This is the start of Kurfürstendamm, the main shopping mile and promenade. To the west it becomes first more elegant and expensive, and then a normal residential street.

Kurfüstendamm in a Day

10:00 am

Start the day with a visit to the **1 Kaiser-Wilhelm-Gedächtniskirche** (Kaiser Wilhelm Memorial Church) (left; ► 118). The new grey church stands beside the ruined tower, which was left as a memorial to peace and reconciliation. Go in, and marvel.

11:00 am

If you've never been to **2 Kaufhaus des Westens** (right; ► 126), the largest department store in Europe, cross the road and walk a short way down Tauentzienstrasse. The quantity and quality of the goods on offer is overwhelming. If you've got children with you who are not yet into shopping, you could take them to the **3 zoo** (► 126) later.

1:00 pm

Time to take a break – either in the Europa-Center or if it's freezing at "Wasserklops" (official name **Weltkugelbrunnen**, below and page 116). Keep an eye on your belongings, if there are a lot of people about.

2:00 pm

Take bus 109 to 4 **Schloss Charlottenburg** (Charlottenburg Palace, above; ➤ 120). It goes along Kurfürstendamm (➤ 123), giving you a preview of your later stroll. After visiting the palace, be sure to take a walk through the park.

4:00 pm

Opposite the palace are the 6 **Ägyptisches Museum** (Egyptian Museum) (left: Nefertiti: ➤ 127) and the 7 **Sammlung Berggruen** (Berggruen Collection; ➤ 128). If you've seen enough, a snack in the Kleine Orangerie (Small Orangery, ➤ 122) will set you up for a stroll along Kudamm.

5:30 pm

Take bus 109 back to Kurfürstendamm. Walk along it and explore the side streets, for example Bleibtreustrasse and Schlüterstrasse, and have a look at the beautiful doorways to the houses.

7:30 pm

Look for a good place to eat. If it's summer and you want to sit outside, you'll be in good company in 8 **Savignyplatz** (➤ 128). It's advisable to book well beforehand, especially at Zwölf Apostel (➤ 130).

Kaiser-Wilhelm-Gedächtniskirche

"All things shall pass" was the text of the sermon preached in the Kaiser Wilhelm Memorial Church on Sunday 22 November, 1943, the day when the dead are commemorated in Germany. A few hours after the service, bombs fell, leaving behind a ruin which has since become famous, an icon of Berlin.

Pomp for Throne and Altar

It would be difficult to invent that sort of symbolism, but there's more. The church was consecrated on 1 September, 1895, the 25th anniversary of the battle of Sedan. Wilhelm II had started an intensive church-building programme. This church, built in honour of his grandfather Wilhelm I, who had died in 1888 at the advanced age of 91, was intended to be the focal point of the new city centre in west Berlin. With its five towers, it was to be the embodiment of the unity of throne and altar, just as his grandfather would have wished. A frieze of Hohenzollern rulers immortalised the family, from Elector Friedrich I to the last Crown Prince Friedrich Wilhelm and his wife Cäcilie.

The Much-loved Hollow Tooth

The west tower, reduced by war damage from 113m to 63m (370 to 206 feet), was soon known to Berliners as the "*hohler Zahn*" (hollow tooth). But Berliners were by no means indifferent to their loss. When the architect Egon Eiermann's plans for a new church proposed demolishing the ruin, a storm of protest broke out. Mountains of letters from outraged readers piled up in newspaper offices.

Grey, with 33,000 Blues

The result is now there to see, for the Senate did not ignore the voice of the people: the ruined tower was retained as a memorial. In 1961, a new chapel, an ascetic grey, flat-fronted octagonal construction, was put up next to the late 19th-century building. The chapel has a hexagonal tower which glows blue in the evening, and then the building attracts attention. It has 33,000 stained-glass panels, made in Chartres in France, almost all in a warm deep blue colour, with a few red, green and yellow panels.

From within, the impression is stunning. The architect clad the chapel's 2.5cm (1-inch) thick walls with a second internal octagonal wall. The gap between the two walls damps

18 Men and a Church

The Kaiser-Wilhelm-Gedächtniskirche actually belongs to 18 Berliners. At the church's consecration the name of a foundation was entered as owner in the land register. A committee of 18 men was established, whose chairman was to be a Prussian prince. According to the committee's statutes it has to maintain the church, make it available to the community and provide good church music at little cost. In recent years the church has become a fashionable burial place for prominent citizens of Berlin.

The stump of the tower and the new building

down the noise from outside and provides space for the lights which illuminate the glass blocks.

Your Cities Are Burnt With Fire

Six bells hang in the new hexagonal church tower, and on the largest are inscribed in German the words of the prophet Isaiah: "Your cities are burnt with fire. But my salvation remains for ever, and my justice shall know no end." In the memorial tower there is a cross made from nails, given by the people of Coventry, in England, whose cathedral was also ruined in the war.

TAKING A BREAK

Take a short walk to **Marché** (➤ 130) and serve yourself.

➕ 194 C3 ✉ Breitscheidplatz 🕐 Church daily 9–7, tower ruin Mon–Sat 10–4:30 🚇 Zoologischer Garten 💶 Church free, tower inexpensive

---

KAISER-WILHELM-GEDÄCHTNISKIRCHE: INSIDE INFO

Top tips Every hour on the hour, the **bells** in the old tower stump ring out a peal written by Prince Louis Ferdinand, the last surviving great-grandson of the last Kaiser.
• At the foot of the new tower the **Eine-Welt-Laden** (One World Shop) demonstrates solidarity with the poor countries of the world.

4 Schloss Charlottenburg

Sophie Charlotte was just 16 when she married the Elector Friedrich of Brandenburg in 1684. He had a rococo palace built for her (1695–9) to the designs of Arnold Nering, which is now the largest and most beautiful in Berlin.

The Elector on a Barge

Andreas Schlüter's equestrian statue of the Great Elector in the main courtyard (1696–7) was, until World War II, on Rathausbrücke in Berlin-Mitte. An attempt was made to take it to safety by boat, but the barge with its precious cargo sank in Tegeler Hafen. It was not until 1950 that the Elector was raised to the surface and, two years later, erected here.

Modelled on Versailles

The original palace was built as a summer retreat for the young queen and was on a far more modest scale than the palace you see today, then consisting only of the central part. Friedrich's growing need for prestige was responsible for the first in a series of additions that saw the palace grow to its present size. In 1701 he had had himself crowned King Friedrich I of Prussia and wanted his new status to be reflected in the grandeur of the building works. Taking the palace of Versailles, in France, as a model, architect Eosander von Göthe was commissioned to lengthen the original house and to add side wings to form a ceremonial courtyard.

18th-century Additions

The great orangery was added as a west wing by Eosander in 1709–12, and in 1710 a tower with a cupola was built on the baroque centre section. In 1740–6 the architect Georg Wenzeslaus von Knobelsdorff added a plain, two-storey new wing on the eastern side, and finally in 1787–91 Carl Gotthard Langhans built a palace theatre, completing the orangery wing. Almost 100 years had passed since the start of the work. Sophie Charlotte was long since dead (in 1705), and the 505m (550-yard) long palace was renamed Schloss Charlottenburg in her memory.

Nothing is the Way It Was

In World War II the palace was badly damaged, and rebuilding did not start until the 1950s. You can now visit the Grosse Eichengalerie (Great Oak Gallery), a banqueting hall with masterly wood-carvings, the Porzellankabinett (Porcelain Gallery) with its valuable collection of Japanese and Chinese pieces, the Weisser Saal (White Hall) and the Goldene Galerie (Golden Gallery). Room after room has been renovated, but nothing is as it used to be. The objects on display consist of pieces from different epochs collected from various Prussian palaces, with others brought in from renovations elsewhere. One room is dedicated to the memory of the Berliner Stadtschloss (City Palace) on Unter den Linden, which had grown since its foundation in 1443 to be the Hohenzollerns' architectural museum and whose ruins were demolished in 1950. German Romantic paintings from the

For Kids
In the palace park, behind the carp pond and the Belvedere, there's a **children's playground** on the banks of the Spree. Outside the park, across Schlossbrücke, there's a jetty for boarding **boat cruises**.

Galerie der Romantik (Gallery of Romanticism), in the new or Knobelsdorff wing, have been moved to the **Alte Nationalgalerie** (▶ 79). Works of art from the dining-room of Potsdamer Stadtschloss have been gathered together in Friedrich II's original residence in the Neue Flügel (New Wing). The former theatre in the orangery wing is the home of the Museum für Vor- und Frühgeschichte (Museum of Pre and Early History). It's most famous exhibits are from Heinrich Schliemann's excavations of Troy.

There are nine feudal residences in the city, all more or less in need of repair. Schloss Charlottenburg has been waiting for years for repairs to the roof, as the faceless statues sunning themselves behind a fence next to the orangery can testify. These actually belong on the roof.

Between Belvedere and Mausoleum

The extensive palace park is a relaxing place to be. Originally it was laid out as a formal French garden, and then at the end of the 18th century, when that was thought to be dated, it was transformed into a landscape garden. Now the original layout is back, but by the carp pond it's less formal, and in the English landscape garden children play, balls and boomerangs fly around and sun-worshippers doze. Queen Luise's **mausoleum**, designed by Karl Friedrich Schinkel as a little Doric temple, is hidden at the end of an avenue of pines. In the **Belvedere**, a tea-house built by Langhans, only the drinking vessels are still to be seen. The classical **Schinkel-Pavillon** (pavilion) evokes thoughts of Italy. In 1824, Friedrich Wilhelm III commissioned it as a simple residence,

Once the master of the house: Friedrich II

SCHLOSS CHARLOTTENBURG: INSIDE INFO

Top tip Find out when palace concerts are performed. Then you can enjoy the splendour of the courtyards as Sophie Charlotte once did.

Hidden gem Stroll up Schlossstrasse to No 69b on the left-hand side of the road. The **Abgusssammlung antiker Plastik** (Collection of Castings of Ancient Statues) doesn't only contain what its name suggests. The ancient works mainly form an exciting backdrop to modern art (Thu–Sun 2–5 pm, admission free).

---

but now it contains only furniture, pictures and sculptures from the 19th century.

TAKING A BREAK

The **Kleine Orangerie** (Small Orangery) at the entrance to the park is a delightful place for a break with a view of the park; in summer the best spot is outside in the garden under ancient trees. At weekends, there are barbecues and musicians provide discreet coffee-house music for entertainment.

🚻 194, west of A5 ✉ Luisenplatz ☎ (030) 32 09 11 🚌 109, 145

Altes Schloss
🕐 Tue–Fri 9–5, Sat–Sun 10–5, guided tours only (last admission 4 pm) 💰 Expensive

Neuer Flügel (Knobelsdorff Wing)
🕐 Mon–Fri 10–6, Sat–Sun 11–6 💰 Moderate

Museum für Vor- und Frühgeschichte
🕐 Tue–Fri 9–5, Sat–Sun 10–5 💰 Moderate; free with *SchauLust* pass (➤ 37)

Schinkel-Pavillon
🕐 Tue–Sun 10–5 (last admission 4:30 pm) 💰 Moderate

Belvedere
🕐 Tue–Sun 10–5, Apr–Oct 💰 Moderate

Mausoleum
🕐 Tue–Sun 10–12 and 1–5 (last admission 4:45 pm), Apr–Oct 💰 Moderate

Park
🕐 Daily 6 am–9 pm, in summer; 6 am–8 pm, in winter 💰 Free

Right: Strolling or people-watching

Welcome to the palace

5 Kurfürstendamm

What is a boulevard? A wide, straight road, an urban highway shaded by trees and bordered with fine houses and businesses, with room to stroll, perhaps 53m (58 yards) wide and 3.5km (just over 2 miles) long – or simply: Kurfürstendamm?

Precisely where Kurfürstendamm starts is hard to say. At Wittenbergplatz with KaDeWe? That's the department store **Kaufhaus des Westens** (➤ 126), a temple to conspicuous consumption, at least worth a visit. But KaDeWe's address is Tauentzienstrasse. So it must be at **Breitscheidplatz**, where Kaiser Wilhelm's ruined church soars skywards. Where street vendors and pavement artists, pickpockets and street performers, pursue their trades. Where customers hold demonstrations and Christians and non Christians celebrate Christmas. Where Joachim Schmettaus's **Weltkugelbrunnen** (World Globe Fountain) is a daily reminder that the globe is split between north and south, and where people meet at "Wasserklops" ➤ 116).

House Numbers

Kurfürstendamm starts at Breitscheidplatz with house No 11. That's because the course of the street was changed and a section renamed. As in many Berlin districts, the numbering of Kudamm runs consecutively down one side of the street, returning down the other side and finishing opposite No 11 with No 237.

The Self-confident West

The **Europa-Center**, 86m (282 feet) and 22 storeys high, was opened in 1965. It is crowned with the revolving 14m (46-foot) high Mercedes star, built to demonstrate to the

East the strength of Capitalism and West Berlin's will to assert itself. This was unmistakably the show-case of the West: 100 shops, restaurants, cafés, theatres, cabarets and offices. Time flows on through a 13m (43-foot) high water-clock.

On the corner of Joachimstaler Strasse a gigantic glass gateau of a building juts out into the cross-roads, with only a red and white striped awning to serve as a reminder of the famous **Café Kranzler**; its original steps have been chopped off. Sitting on the balcony of the café-bar, you are informed of the latest market trends by enormous charts on Berlin's largest advertisement display. Nobody should think that time has stood still in west Berlin, just because they're building in the east of the city.

Little more than decoration: Café Kranzler

Beautiful Side-streets

The side-streets with their luxuriant trees and cosmopolitan flair are the best thing about Kurfürstendamm. The **Meineckestrasse** has good restaurants, and **Fasanenstrasse** has its Wintergartensensemble: a group of beautiful Berlin villas like the **Literaturhaus**. Next to this there's a delightful restaurant garden (▶ 130) and down some steps a good bookshop. At the end of the

The New West of the City

Bismarck had the Parisian Champs-Élysées in mind when he had the road which, since the 16th century, had linked the Stadtschloss with the hunting lodge in Grunewald extended into a boulevard. At the end of the 19th century the emancipated middle-class moved into what was then the new west end of the city and built houses with smart façades. At the back, Berlin artists lived in so-called garden houses, small one- or two-room dwellings. It's a long time since an artist could afford one! Any surviving columns, cherubs or art nouveau work serve now to adorn lawyers' and dentists' practices.

1960s these houses were to be pulled down to make way for an urban motorway; determined resistence saved them. Take time to look at the marble doorways in **Uhlandstrasse** and stroll through the pretty shops in the **Bleibtreustrasse**. And how quiet and peaceful it is when you get to **Ludwigkirchplatz**.

Everyone has a job in life

Moving Up-market

Between Uhlandstrasse and Knesebeckstrasse, in the Kurfürstendamm-Karree, you can explore the multimedia **"Story of Berlin"**. To the north lies **Savignyplatz** (➤ 128), surrounded by fashion stores, small restaurants and specialist firms. Schlüterstrasse has chic little dress shops, and on Kurfürstendamm it's gradually getting more and more classy and expensive: there are no price labels to help you decide! If you turn right into Leibnizstrasse and then again into the Kolonnaden, you might think you're in a relic from old Prussia. But in fact **Walter-Benjamin-Platz** is brand new, it just looks old. Further to the west, beyond **Olivaer Platz** and finally beyond **Adenauer Platz**, Kurfürstendamm quickly becomes a residential street with greengrocers', bakers' and grocers' shops. But the side streets are another matter…

Noblesse of yesteryear

TAKING A BREAK

There are many possibilities. **Soup-Kultur** (Kurfürstenstrasse 224, corner of Meineckestrasse) has delicious things: cream soup with cider, *borscht*, or potato and ginger soup. **Einhorn** (Wittenbergplatz 5/6) has very tasty vegetarian snacks.

Guten Appetit!

✚ 194 A3–C3

The Story of Berlin

✉ Kurfürstendamm 207 ☎ (030) 88 72 01 00 🕐 Daily 10–8 (last admission 6 pm)
🚇 Uhlandstrasse 💰 Expensive

KURFÜRSTENDAMM: INSIDE INFO

Top tips The **Käthe-Kollwitz-Museum**, the only privately owned museum in the city, exhibits socially critical and political drawings by Kollwitz (1867–1945), along with her entire work in sculpture (Fasanenstrasse 24, tel: (030) 882 52 10, Wed–Mon 11–6, admission moderate).

• **E-mails** can be sent 24 hours a day from the internet café easyEverything – at least one of the 340 PCs is bound to be free (Kurfürstendamm 224, corner of Meineckestrasse).

• Art lovers will find **galleries** in the passage between Fasanenstrasse 29 and Uhlandstrasse, and in Mommsenstrasse and Niebuhrstrasse.

• For a particularly classy (and costly) haircut, try Berlin's celebrity hairstylist Udo Walz on the Kempinski-Plaza (Uhlandstrasse 181, tel: (030) 882 74 57).

At Your Leisure

❷ KaDeWe

Saucepans or caviar, pins or high fashion, you can get it all, and in many different varieties, in the KaDeWe (Kaufhaus des Westens) department store. The high point is the legendary fine foods floor, a mecca for gourmets and beloved of the public, although you need to be extraordinarily decisive in order to choose between 1,300 sorts of cheese, 1,200 sausage and ham specialities, and 400 kinds of bread and rolls. The only greater challenge is the one confronting wine-lovers faced with 2,400 labels from every continent. The fish department bears comparison with many an aquarium: the tanks hold, according to season, swarms of sturgeon, pike, catfish, carp, perch and trout. Seafood of all sorts spends a short time here before it disappears into the kitchens of first-class hotels and restaurants.

You can take the easy way out, and after you have visited the 7,000sq m (over 8,000 square yards) of the delicatessen department – the largest in Europe – you can sample the skills of 150 cooks and pastry-makers. International gourmet food companies like Bocuse and Cipriani have outlets here and they don't just serve canapés on their stalls (stands). Or you can take the panoramic lift up through the central atrium to the eighth floor, where you can eat in the glass-domed restaurant high above the roofs of Berlin.

When it opened in 1907, on the edge of the then affluent west of the city, the store was already a talking-point. In 1943 an American plane crashed into the central atrium and practically demolished it; two storeys were rebuilt and reopened in 1950. After the fall of the Berlin Wall in November 1989, when everybody was only interested in the new city centre, KaDeWe increased in size again, this time to 60,000sq m (nearly 72,000 square yards), so that it is once again the largest department store in Europe. The number and extent of its departments are still breathtaking. Be it Versace or Valentino, Meissen china or fine perfumes, neckties or cosmetics, it's all here. Have you got your children with you, or a car, or a dog? Are you too warmly dressed? No problem. The children will be looked after (and a pager provided for the parents), the dog goes into the kennels, the car into the car-park (parking lot), your coat into the cloakroom (checkroom). The present you bought for Australian friends will be sent for you, you can borrow a roof-rack to transport the carpet, the suitcase will be put in store. Are you sure you had a problem?

➕ 194 C3 ✉ Tauentzienstrasse 21–24 ☎ (030) 21 21 22 89 🕔 Mon–Fri 9:30–8, Sat 9–8 🚇 Wittenbergplatz

❸ Zoologischer Garten

At Zoologischer Garten station you can already smell the camels, and even if in summer the thick foliage shuts off the view from the car-park (parking lot), you know at once that you are in the right place. There will of course always be a longish queue (line) at the Löwentor (Lion Gate) entrance to the zoo, because Berliners visit the zoo as often as they would their favourite aunt. You'll find them there in droves, be it to sympathise with the elephant's two-year pregnancy, or rejoice at the birth of the 80kg infant (176 pounds). When Knautschke, a legendary hippopotamus which had survived the war, died hundreds of thousands mourned. They are starting to get impatient with Yan Yan (Sweetie), the stand-offish panda, though. The prudish Chinese female has been eating for two, chomping on bamboo stems from the south of France since 1995, but refuses to reproduce.

When, at the suggestion of Alexander von Humboldt and the landscape architect Peter Joseph Lenné, Berlin zoo was founded in 1844, it was the first zoo in Germany. The initial stock came from Emperor Friedrich Wilhelm IV's menagerie on the Pfaueninsel (Peacock Island) on the Havel river.

The aquarium with its more than 10,000 animals was founded and directed by the zoologist Alfred Brehm. In the half-dark you feel as though you are under water. The archerfish shoots down a midge, and the electric eel really quivers – to scare off its enemies and there are hammer-headed sharks and crocodiles.

It was thanks to the director Katharina Heinroth that the zoo, whose collection had been reduced to a mere 91 animals at the end of World War II, could be built up again. Now more than 1,400 species live here.

There is another zoo, with five times the area, at Friedrichsfelde in the east of the city. Since 1955 it has been maintained by thousands of volunteers.

☐ 194 C4 ☒ Hardenbergplatz 8 (Löwentor), Budapester Strasse 34 (Aquarium, Elefantentor) ☎ (030) 25 40 10 ◷ Daily 9–5, Nov–Mar; 9–6:30, Apr–Sep; 9–6, Oct. Aquarium daily 9–6 ◉ Zoologischer Garten ◍ Expensive

❻ Ägyptisches Museum

She is so beautiful that visitors move around and around her as though in a dream, and many come only to see her – Nefertiti. Her left eye is missing so you could be forgiven for thinking that she is winking. Many people are disappointed to learn that this limestone bust from the workshop of Tutmosis is not a true image of an Egyptian queen from over 3,300 years ago but an ideal of beauty. She is, so to speak, a decoy, enticing art-lovers to look at other exhibits. As soon as visitors enter the museum, when they have no eyes for the competition, they are met by the colossal statues of the ancient Egyptian goddess of war, Sakhmet, with her lions' heads. In due course these treasures from the time of

Just take it easy!

Yesterday's architecture for Picasso's modern art

Akhenaten will arrive on Museumsinsel (➤ 78).

🏛 194, west of A5 ✉ Schlossstrasse 70 ☎ (030) 34 35 73 11 🕐 Tue–Sun 10–6 🚍 109, 145 💶 Moderate; free with *SchauLust* pass (➤ 37)

🐧 Sammlung Berggruen

The works of Picasso and his contemporaries – Paul Klee, Georges Braque and Giacometti – are exhibited in this collection, which the returned emigrant Heinz Berggruen, art-collector and friend of Picasso, first loaned and finally donated to his native city. This is how Berlin came by a priceless Picasso collection, with 69 paintings, drawings and sculptures grouped round *Le chandail jaune* (*Dora*), a portrait of the artist's mistress, the writer and photographer Dora Maar.

Also on display are objects of African tribal art, which go surprisingly well with the modern and cubist paintings.

🏛 194, west of A5 ✉ Schlossstrasse 1 ☎ (030) 326 95 80 🕐 Tue–Fri 10–6, Sat–Sun 11–6 🚍 109, 145 💶 Moderate; free with *SchauLust* pass (➤ 37)

🐧 Savignyplatz

At first glance Savignyplatz is just a small patch of green on either side of broad Kantstrasse. But this truly urban centre of Berlin's West End is made up of all the narrow streets which come together at this square. In fact, in the consciousness of west Berliners, the whole district with its exquisite small shops, beautiful houses and dozens of vibrant restaurants and bars is considered to be part of the Savignyplatz. Stroll here on warm summer evenings and you'll see that the restaurants have spread their tables out onto the pavements (sidewalks).

People drink, laugh and chat under ancient trees, sometimes until dawn. Those late-night revellers who have not yet gone home may be slumped in the legendary Zwiebelfisch (➤ 132) or are already on their way to the Schwarzes Café (➤ 130), where they can have breakfast at any hour.

🏛 194 A3 🚉 Savignyplatz

Where to...
Eat and Drink

Prices

Prices given are for one person, excluding drinks.
€ under 12 euros €€ 12–25 euros €€€ over 25 euros

Diekmann €€

A general store's shelves of boxes stacked up to the ceiling, and plates decorated with pictures of the groceries, are all evidence of the history of this place. The snowy white table-cloths and neatly folded napkins also suggest an earlier age. Everything is served to perfection. The lunch-time menu is exceptionally good value.

➕ 194 B3 ⊠ Meineckestrasse 7 ☎ (030) 883 33 21 🕔 Mon–Sat noon–1 am, Sun 4 pm–1 am

Florian €–€€

When the film festival was still held in West Berlin, celebrities often came here, and many stars have remained true to this Franconian cooking (from northern Bavaria). They still serve roasts with *sauerkraut* after 11 pm.

➕ 194 A4 ⊠ Grolmanstrasse 52 ☎ (030) 313 91 84 🕔 Daily 6 pm–3 am

Hard Rock Café €

A gleaming half-Cadillac is mounted over the entrance, and inside is the Trabant that once belonged to the band U2. Fans can see one of German rock band Tote Hosen's shirts and one of Elton John's suits and enjoy their fast-food accompanied by the eponymous rock music.

➕ 194 B3 ⊠ Meineckestrasse 21 ☎ (030) 88 46 20 🕔 Daily noon–2 am

Kabir €€

If you are looking for good vegetarian Indian cuisine, you can't go wrong here. Food is well spiced, just as the customers like it.

➕ 194 A4 ⊠ Carmerstrasse 17 ☎ (030) 312 81 57 🕔 Mon–Fri noon–midnight, Sat–Sun noon–1 am

Kuchi €–€€

The marvellous inexpensive lunch menu has Japanese fish-balls, *yakitori* dishes and other delicacies. In the evening it's packed full.

➕ 194 B3 ⊠ Kantstrasse 30 ☎ (030) 31 50 78 15 🕔 Mon–Thu noon–midnight, Fri–Sun 12:30 pm–12:30 am, lunch menu Mon–Sat noon–5 pm

Lubitsch €–€€

The stucco on the ceiling, mirrors on the walls (making the room look bigger) and, above all, a modern cuisine ensure that this place is one of the most popular in the area. For lunch there's always a choice of vegetarian and meat dishes and pasta.

➕ 194 A3 ⊠ Bleibtreustrasse 47 ☎ (030) 882 37 56 🕔 Mon–Sat 9:30 am–1 am, Sun 5 pm–1 am, lunch menu Mon–Sat noon–6 pm

Manzini €€

Marble below, Murano glass above, that's the sort of elegance which media people go for in old West Berlin, and it's done particularly well here. The bistro-style cooking is excellent – at last a real Italian risotto as it should be cooked and served – so you can be sure of an enjoyable evening.

➕ 194 A2 ⊠ Ludwigkirchstrasse 11 ☎ (030) 885 78 20 🕔 Daily 8 am–2 am, meals served noon–midnight, lunch menu Mon–Fri noon–3 pm

Marché €

Marché is self-service. There are around 30 hot and cold international dishes to choose from.

╬ 194 C3 ⊠ Kurfürstendamm 14/15 ☎ (030) 882 75 78 Ⓞ Daily 8 am– midnight, meals served 11:30 am– 11:30 pm

Opera Italiana €

Is Schloss Charlottenburg (▶ 120–2) really in Naples? Opposite it, anyway, you can eat surrounded by little houses in Italian streets, with washing on the line and plenty of images of saints – all as a backdrop for freshly made pasta, enormous pizzas and Rucola ravioli.

╬ 194, west of A5 ⊠ Spandauer Damm 5 ☎ (030) 34 70 36 26 Ⓞ Daily noon–midnight, lunch menu Mon–Fri 2–4

Wellenstein €€

At Wellenstein, experience city flair from breakfast (served until 6 pm!) onwards. You will find newspapers to read, discreet music and a well-dressed clientele. The menu is varied and prices are reasonable.

╬ 194 A3 ⊠ Kurfürstendamm 190 ☎ (030) 881 78 50 Ⓞ Daily 9 am–3 am

Wintergarten €€

The best seats are in the garden of the Literaturhaus or at least at a table overlooking the entrance. The hollow-cheeked pallid poets of yesteryear have long since departed, but this idyllic place, which lies just two minutes from Kurfürstendamm, has since suffered the fate of all betrayed secrets: it's always too late. The cooking uses ingredients from organic sources.

╬ 194 B3 ⊠ Fasanenstrasse 2 ☎ (030) 882 54 14 Ⓞ Daily 9:30 am–1 am

Zum Hugenotten €€€

Day after day the head chef proves that this restaurant on the 13th floor of the Hotel Interconti, high above the roofs of Berlin, is one of the best in town. You pay for that, but the wonderful view over the new and old city centres is free.

╬ 194 C3 ⊠ Budapester Strasse 2 ☎ (030) 26 02 12 63 Ⓞ Mon–Sat 6–11 pm, last orders 10:30 pm

Zwölf Apostel €€€

Images of the 12 Apostles sit high up on the walls; the pizzas are named after them. Bring an appetite: the pizzas are thin, crispy – and huge.

╬ 194 A3 ⊠ Bleibtreustrasse 49 (Passage) ☎ (030) 312 14 33 Ⓞ Daily 9 am–1 am

CAFÉS

Aedes

You can eat breakfast at any hour of the day, so long as it's French (croissants) or Italian (tramezzini). Or you can have antipasti with a glass of red wine. A metropolitan ambience is provided by the S-Bahn rattling past overhead.

╬ 194 A3 ⊠ Savignyplatz, S-Bahn-bogen 599 ☎ (030) 31 50 95 35 Ⓞ Daily 10 am–1 am

Hardenberg

This student café near the Technical University is often full and usually noisy. Those weary of the city can daydream undisturbed.

╬ 194 B4 ⊠ Hardenbergstrasse 10 ☎ (030) 312 26 44 Ⓞ Sun–Thu 9 am–1 am, Fri–Sat 9 am–2 am

Leysieffer

Anyone on a diet should give a wide berth to this place. Specialities include rich cream cakes and walnut ice-cream with plum sauce.

╬ 194 B3 ⊠ Kurfürstendamm 218 ☎ (030) 885 74 80 Ⓞ Mon–Sat 10–8, Sun 11–7

Schwarzes Café

When the interior was black, many customers were reluctant to leave the sunlight for such a dark hole. That has changed, but it still has a legend-ary reputation, whether for breakfast, lunch or a beer and cocktails.

╬ 194 B3 ⊠ Kantstrasse 148 ☎ (030) 313 80 38 Ⓞ 3 am–10 am, otherwise 24-hour

Where to... Shop

AROUND KURFÜRSTENDAMM

When the **Europa-Center** was built in 1965, it was one of the first shopping centres in West Germany, and it still has a wide selection of goods in all price ranges: watches, jewellery, cosmetics and toys. There are fashion houses here – Esprit, Görtz (for shoes) St Germain and Orsay, and Spanish fashion chain Zara is at Kurfürstendamm 236. The **Neuen Kranzlereck** (Kurfürstendamm 19–24) also has mainly fashion stores, from Gerry Weber via Strauss Innovation to Mango and Karstadt Sport.

In the **Perlen-Bar** (Uhlandstrasse 156) you can buy everything you need to make your own personalised jewellery. Fortunately, they also have

ready-made items. **Paint Your Style** (Bleibtreustrasse 46) also challenges the creativity of customers: daily from 11 am to 10 pm you can paint your own plates and cups. The job has been done for you if you buy azulejos (hand-painted tiles from Portugal) at **Kachelatelier Ulrike Pohl** (Leibnizstrasse 47).

Patrick Hellmann (Bleibtreustrasse 20) stocks classy clothes from Armani to Dior. **Nice Price** (Knesebeckstrasse 8–9), on the other hand, has designer jeans at half price. **Secondo** (Mommsenstrasse 61) sells second-hand clothes with fashionable labels. **Roserosa** (Bleibtreustrasse 48) has fine underwear, **Bleibgrün** (Bleibtreustrasse 29–30) avant garde shoes, and **Gangart** (Mommsenstrasse 45) ecologically sound ones. High-class shops like **Jil Sander** (Kurfürstendamm 185) cluster round Olivaer Platz. **Moda Mo** (Giesebrechtstrasse 17) will fit you out for that glamorous evening. Every make of model car – at a scale

of 1:18 – can be bought at **Modellautos Dieter Platzer** (Leibnizstrasse 40).

AROUND SAVIGNYPLATZ

The designer store **Stilwerk** (Kantstrasse 17, corner of Uhlandstrasse) has everything imaginable for making your home more beautiful: exotic indoor plants, hi-fi equipment from Bang & Olufsen and Bechstein, antiques and expensive espresso machines, but also ethnic knick-knacks. Bargain hunters won't find anything here. Many smaller shops also stock luxury goods. **Schlafwandel** (Kantstrasse 21) has heaps of good things for the bathroom and bedroom. **lalaine** (Kantstrasse 145) sells wool and haberdashery, as well as clothing made from natural fibres. **Cover b** (Knesebeckstrasse 76) has handbags designed in-house. Be it Rameses or Friedrich II, **Berliner Zinnfiguren** (Knesebeckstrasse 88) has a lead

model of him (or her, of course). You'll find imported delicacies and own-make chocolates (truffles with garlic) at **Confiserie Melanie** (Goethestrasse 4).

The intellectual centre of west Berlin has long been here. Among the many bookshops, **Bücherbogen**, right on Savignyplatz (S-Bahn arch 593), is a treasure house of works on architecture, art, design and photography. **Galerie 2000** (Knesebeckstrasse 56/58) is the epitome of art and architecture shops. Lovers of poetry should be sure to visit **Autorenbuchhandlung** (Carmerstrasse 10), which has the largest selection of poetry in any German-speaking country. **Andenbuch** (Goethestrasse 69) has literature from Spain and Latin-America, while **Prinz Eisenherz** (Bleibtreustrasse 52) has gay and lesbian works. **Antiquariat Schwarz** (Carmerstrasse 11) is a prime address for all those who like rummaging through old books hoping to make a find.

Where to be... Entertained

THEATRE AND MUSIC

Lovers of good acting and choreography are well catered for at **Schaubühne am Lehniner Platz** (Kurfürstendamm 153, tel: (030) 89 00 23), converted from a 1920s Expressionist-style cinema. **Renaissance-Theater** (Hardenbergstrasse 6, tel: (030) 312 42 02) is a beautiful art nouveau building where modern plays are performed.

Performances in the mirrored tent of **Bar jeder Vernunft** (Schaperstrasse 24, tel: (030) 883 15 82) offer some of the best entertainment going. **Stachelschweine** (Europa-Center, tel: (030) 261 47 95) has over the years lost some of its cabaret bite. **Komödie** (Kurfürstendamm 206, tel: (030) 88 59 11 88) and **Theater am Kudamm** (Kurfürstendamm 206–209, tel: (030) 88 59 11 88) are also devoted to light comedy, farce and popular theatre.

Quasimodo, next to the *fin de siècle* Theater des Westens, underneath the Delphi cinema (Kantstrasse 12a, tel: (030) 312 80 86), is a legend in Berlin, putting on live jazz and blues. **A-Trane** (Bleibtreustrasse 1, tel: (030) 313 25 50) has modern jazz or swing almost every evening. In **Soultrane** in the Stilwerk store (Kantstrasse 17, corner of Uhlandstrasse, tel: (030) 31 51 50) you can dine almost every evening to the sound of jazz, and on Sundays there's a jazz brunch.

BARS

Around Kurfürstendamm there's a good selection of places which have had time to establish their own individual image. Art lovers especially gather at cocktail time in **Galerie Bremer** (Fasanenstrasse 37, tel: (030) 881 49 08, Mon–Sat 8 pm–2 am). **Zur weissen Maus** (Ludwigkirchplatz 12, tel: (030) 88 67 92 88, daily 8 pm–4 am) is the meeting-place for the area's intellectuals. For years night-owls from yuppies to gays have chosen to spend the small hours by **Zufall** (Pfalzburger Strasse 10, tel: (030) 883 24 37, Wed–Sun from 11 pm). Probably the most famous Berlin night-spot is **Paris Bar** (Kantstrasse 152, tel: (030) 313 80 52, daily noon–2 am). Journalists have written long appreciative articles, and now there's even a book about this institution. It looks like an art gallery, has a number of illustrious customers and is proud of its French-speaking waiters. Its continuing success has led to the creation of an off-shoot in the next-door house: **Le Bar du Paris Bar**.

Actors – and exhibitionists – have their nightly stage at **Diener** (Grolmanstrasse 47, tel: (030) 881 53 29, daily from 6 pm), which is an inn left over from a two-storey riding-school established in 1893: "Tattersall des Westens". The walls have probably not been painted for 50 years – the place is famous for it. It's not a bar, more a dive, as is **Zwiebelfisch** (Savignyplatz 7/8, tel: (030) 312 73 63, daily noon–6 am), the domain of the now older 68ers (1968, the year of student unrest in Germany) and their sympathisers of all ages.

Non-smokers should at all costs avoid **Times Bar** in the Hotel Savoy (Fasanenstrasse 9, tel: (030) 31 10 30) – years ago this classic bar set up a Casa del Habano for cigar-smokers. There's a walk-in humidor (a room for keeping cigars moist), and expert advice is on offer.

Kreuzberg

Getting Your Bearings

A multicultural melting pot, riots in the shadow of the Wall – for years that was West Germans' image of Kreuzberg. When the Wall fell, the impoverished "alternative" area found itself in the middle of the city. Gradually the former destination of choice for young people became the latest place for everyone to be.

Checkpoint Charlie
KOCH- STR.
Kochstr.
Bundes-druckerei
Wald-eckpark
ORANIEN-
STR.
HENRIETTE-HEINE-STR.
WILHELM-
STR.
STRESEMANN-
STR.
MORITZ-PLATZ
Moritzplatz
ORANIEN-
PLA
Th.-Wolff-Park
STR.
LINDEN-
4 Jüdisches Museum
KREUZ-
C
HALLESCHES
TEMPELHOFER
MEHRINGPLATZ
Patentamt
Prinzenstr.
WASSERTOR-PLATZ
Hallesches Tor
GITSCHINER
STR.
SKALI
UFER
GITSCHINER STR.
WATERLOO
DAMM
UFER
BLÜCHER-PL
STR.
Böckler-park
BERG
Mehring-damm
BLÜCHER-UFER
PRINZEN-
Landwehrkanal
Rathaus
Friedhof
HORNSTR.
YORCK-
STR.
STR.
URBAN-
BLÜCHER-
0   400 m
GNEISENAU-
Gneisenaustr.
WALD-
STR.
0   400 yar.
7 Riehmers Hofgarten
ZOSSENER
KORTESTR.
BERG-
STR.
BERGMANN-
STR.
Südstern
5 Bergmann-strasse
MARHEINEKE-PL
BAER-
SÜDSTERN
HASEN-HEIDE
MEHRING-
BERGMANN-
STR.
FRIESEN-
Viktoria-park
CHAMISSO-PL
Friedhöfe
6

Kreuzberg is now one half of the new district Kreuzberg-Friedrichshain. The Spree divides former West Berlin from former East Berlin here, and the Oberbaum bridge re-connects them. Refrigeration plants and warehouses are being converted into media factories and lofts. Plans for "Music City", "Spreesinus" and "Media Spree" comprise high-rise and glass palaces. At East Side Gallery, between Oberbaum and Schilling bridges, vast new building works are about to start. Kreuzberg was also chosen to be the location for Daniel Libeskind's flamboyant Jewish Museum.

That doesn't mean, though, that the old Kreuzberg has disappeared. Here you will find the largest Turkish community outside Turkey, with its own banks and jewellery shops right next to vibrant bars and off-beat cafés. The

Right: Berlin's most beautiful bridge, Oberbaumbrücke gives a great view of Berlin-Mitte

Page 133: Beautiful façades, carefully restored

Oranienstrasse is still the alternative Kudamm, even if squatters have become home-owners and good restaurants welcome guests from other districts.

Artists are coming back from the now up-market and expensive Berlin-Mitte and the Bergmannstrasse is the centre of the district's bohemian scene. There's still room for everyone who wants to be in Kreuzberg.

Kreuzberg has a big-city feel by the Spree but a small-town feel by the Landwehrkanal. It's impoverished in the north but elegant in the south, but its imaginative style is ubiquitous.

Kreuzberg in a Day

10:00 am

Start your day at **1 Oberbaumbrücke** (Oberbaum bridge) (➤ 138–40), Berlin's most beautiful bridge. If you want a photo of the East Side Gallery (above), now's the time, because the light is perfect. Move swiftly out of noisy Skalitzer Strasse, turning into friendly Muskauer Strasse, which leads to Mariannenplatz – scene of legendary May Day riots – and to the cultural complex of **2 Künstlerhaus Bethanien** (➤ 147).

12:00 noon

Stroll on to Heinrichplatz. If you like, drop into the Rote Harfe (➤ 142), the former meeting place of revolutionary groups protesting against the establishment.

1:00 pm

Spend an hour or so browsing the eclectic shops on 🖪 **Oranienstrasse** (➤ 141–2) and soaking up the area's multicultural atmosphere.

2:00 pm

Take the U-Bahn to Hallesches Tor from Kottbusser Tor (don't be put off by the heavy police presence here, keeping an eye out for drug dealers and other miscreants). Then take a bus (240) or walk to Lindenstrasse and the imposing 🖪 **Jüdisches Museum** (Jewish Museum, right; ➤ 143–6), which celebrates 2,000 years of German-Jewish history.

4:30 pm

Take U-Bahn train No 6 one stop to Mehringdamm station, then change onto the U7. Travel one stop to Gneisenaustrasse station. From here Zossener Strasse leads directly to Marheinekeplatz and 🖪 **Bergmannstrasse** (➤ 145–6) with its shops, cafés and restaurants.

6:00 pm

If you would like to see a bit of greenery: just behind Mehringdamm is the start of one of the most beautiful city parks, the 🖪 **Viktoriapark** (left; ➤ 147). The rear courtyards in Yorckstrasse can be really elegant, as you can see at 🖪 **Riehmers Hofgarten** (➤ 147).

8:00 pm

Exhausted? In summer, book a table at Osteria No 1 (➤ 148), where you'll certainly feel as though you were in Italy. Afterwards, you might like to go dancing at Golgatha (➤ 152), to find out just how long Kreuzberg nights can be.

❶ Oberbaumbrücke

On one side the Fernsehturm (➤ 84) dominates the skyline, on the other silvery giants wrestle in the water, and the odd large warehouse is a reminder that these used to be docklands – this is almost the geographical centre of the city.

A Florentine Bridge for Berlin

Between Oberbaum and Schilling bridges – looking across to the city centre – a concrete stump sticks out of the water. This is the solitary remnant of Brommy Bridge, blown up in 1945. A new construction is planned, which will not only span the Spree but also contain a hotel and a disco or fitness studio, all in a glass edifice built next to the roadway over the water. It was designed by the Berlin architect Gerhard Spangenberg, modelled on the Ponte Vecchio which crosses the River Arno in Florence, and the Rialto bridge in Venice. Perhaps Berlin will soon have a new Brommy Bridge.

The striking red-brick bridge with its twin towers, crossed by the yellow U-Bahn and brightly coloured cars, gives the impression of being playful yet defiant. Beneath it boats, pleasure steamers and barges sail past on the Spree. Oberbaum bridge was built in 1896 to the designs of the chief government architect Otto Stahn; badly damaged in World War II, it was open only to pedestrians until its restoration in the mid-1990s. More than 500 different kinds of tile were used in the restored bridge. The elegant steel arch, which replaces the missing central arcades, was designed in 1992 by the Portuguese architect Santiago Calatrava. The two towers with their pointed capping, inspired by the Prenzlauer town gate, are a reference to the original function of the bridge as a toll station. Formerly a wooden beam – the "Oberbaum" – barred access to the city at night.

A view from the bridge at night – of the industrial townscape of Friedrichshain

East Side Gallery

In autumn 1990, the wall on the eastern side of the Spree, which for 1.3km (0.75 miles) blocks the view of the river from Mühlenstrasse, was transformed by 110 artists from 40 countries into an open-air gallery. The East Side Gallery still expresses the euphoric and world-wide participation in the fall of the Wall, though wind and rain are gradually taking the colour out of the pictures, several of which have already been repainted. The best known are the *Bruderkuss* (*Fraternal Kiss*) by Dimitri Vrubel, which shows Soviet president Brezhnev and GDR president Honecker embracing, and Birgit Kinder's wall-piercing *Trabi* (based on the notorious GDR car, the Trabant).

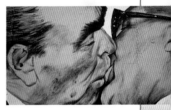

Friedrichshain

To the south of the bridge, three giants – *Molecule Men* by Jonathan Borofsky – symbolise the districts of Kreuzberg, Friedrichshain and Treptow, whose boundaries meet here. Friedrichshain, the neglected GDR working-class (blue-collar) quarter, has developed in the past few years, with its squatters and rows of bars on Simon-Dachstrasse and Wühlischstrasse, into the meeting-place for young Berliners, a replacement for Spandauer Vorstadt, which has become too grand.

Off the Beaten Track

A quarter of an hour's walk down the Schlesische Strasse, after the filling station, a narrow alley runs off to the left-hand side, which belongs to waterside restaurant **Freischwimmer** (Vor dem Schlesisches Tor 2, tel: (030) 61 07 43 09, open from noon). The former boat-house and store rooms have become the kitchen and bar, and there is a floating outdoor platform where you can relax with a drink. It's a very beautiful place to be, and on the other bank you can see members of the Club der Visionäre in their comfortable chairs.

Setting the Tone

With more than 1,000 rock and pop bands, ten famous classical orchestras, more than 200 choirs and over 250 musical venues, Berlin has become the musical centre of Germany. All the same, the number of stars is not great. The best known German artistes include Herbert Grönemeyer, Die Ärzte, Rosenstolz, Blixa Bargeld's Einstürzende Neubauten and 2raum-Wohnung. Curiously, of all people, it was the notorious East Berlin rock band Rammstein which was the first German-speaking band to gain a gold disc for sales in the USA.

The U-Bahn station Schlesisches Tor is no longer the terminus of Line 1

The Kreuzberg Mélange

Commercial and residential premises side by side are part of the traditional Kreuzberg mélange, which is spreading out on both sides of the Spree. Various media enterprises have moved into empty warehouses and a redundant egg refrigeration plant; Oberbaum-City has been created out of a bankrupt light-bulb factory and Kreuzberg has profited from the trend towards new trade premises and lofts. Employees of Universal Deutschland, the country's biggest music company, which has moved its HQ from Hamburg to the banks of the Spree, talk enthusiastically about the splendid new location, as do the producers of the music programme MTV.

TAKING A BREAK

The Universal-Kantine at the water's edge has become the **Fritz Fischer** restaurant (Stralauer Allee 1). From here you can contemplate *Molecule Men* sparkling in the sun, wave to people on pleasure cruisers, and learn from the loudspeaker commentaries that you are sitting in front of a former egg refrigeration plant.

➕ 198 C3 ◉ Schlesisches Tor

OBERBAUMBRÜCKE: INSIDE INFO

Top tip Under the U-Bahn station Schlesisches Tor, on the opposite side from Oberbaumbrücke, **Kaufhaus Kato** puts on concerts, plays and exhibitions. It's open only for events (tel: (030) 611 23 39).

3 Oranienstrasse

For years "new Berliners" from anywhere between Anatolia and Swabia didn't come just to Berlin but specifically to Kreuzberg or even to SO 36, the postal district of southeast Kreuzberg, between the Wall, the Spree and the Landwehr-kanal – cheap, colourful and cheerful. "O-strasse", as it's known here, is its centre.

Refugees

The first inhabitants settled here in the 17th century; they were sectarian refugees, Huguenots from the French province of Orange. In 1849 the street was named after their homeland, the principality of Oranien. It developed into a good shopping street, the "eastern Kurfürstendamm". This was brought to an end by the Nazi era, World War II and the Wall. From the early 1960s, migrant workers from eastern Turkey moved into the cheap accommodation. Students, artists and the impoverished had already settled in by the start of the "economic miracle" of the 1950s.

SO 36 still exists. It's now the name of a former house in Oranienstrasse (No. 190) which is the place for night-life (➤ 152). "Café Fatal" is the title of the Sunday tea-dance, the Monday party is the "Electric Ballroom", "Hungrige Herzen" (Hungry Hearts) is a gay-lesbian event, as is "Gayhane" – but this time with Turkish pop music. But such multicultural events are only a part of the life of Oranienstrasse. Across the neighbouring courtyard is the entrance to the mosque.

Turkish Muslim mothers, swathed in long dark robes and head-scarves, lead their extended families through the streets. It's doubtful whether they approve of the girl next door's pierced nose and eyebrows any more than the punks' red and green hair. The organic food shop Kraut und Rüben is run by a women's collective. Next to the kebab shop convertibles can be hired for the weekend, so young men can spend a couple of days ogling a Jaguar. There are dressmakers' and delis, bars next door to dress-shops and a gallery, which resisted the attractions of a location in the new Berlin-Mitte area.

Below: The Turkish market on the Maybachufer

Bottom: Shoe shop at Paul-Lincke-Ufer 44

In Bierhimmel (➤ 152) cream cakes soothe the pangs of love – and hunger, and in the family garden an inexpensive Turkish lunch is served. From shops which advertise their wares in Turkish and Arabic you can phone any country you like at reasonable rates. Banks and jewellers' seem to expect only Turkish customers. After all, they make up 33 per cent of the population.

Schokoladenfabrik

The "Chocolate Factory" – a meeting-place for women from across the globe

End of the Line for Revolutionaries

The strategic centre, in Heinrichplatz, has famous bars like **Zum Elefanten** and **Rote Harfe**. It was here that, in the 1970s, schemes were hatched to thwart the Senate's plans to clean up the district and disperse the occupants of the inner courtyards. Half of all Berlin's squats were in Kreuzberg. This is where barricades were built and tourist busses were bombarded with stones, until a so-called cautious urban renewal began. New developments are being sympathetically slotted in to the area, retaining its essential character.

TAKING A BREAK

The **Bateau Ivre** (Oranienstrasse 18) serves good cakes and a delicious breakfast, to the accompaniment of traditional French *chansons*. It's also a wonderful place to sit outside and watch the world go by.

In summer, life in Kreuzberg goes on outside

✚ 197 D3–F3   Ⓢ Görlitzer Bahnhof

ORANIENSTRASSE: INSIDE INFO

Top tips The shining cobbles on the corner of Oranienstrasse and Skalitzer Strasse are **brass plaques** installed by the artist Gunter Demnig in memory of the 1,300 murdered Jews who lived in Kreuzberg.

• On the Paul-Lincke-Ufer by the Landwehrkanal there are rows of little **cafés and restaurants** with beautiful gardens.

• Every Tuesday and Friday from noon to 6 pm, the **Turkish market** on the Maybachufer offers fresh fish, bread and cakes, fruit and vegetables, buttons, fabrics, soap, tea-glasses...

• The "image-factory" DIM (Oranienstrasse 26) makes strange objects out of brushes from the workshop for the blind.

• Women of every nationality meet in Hamam, the **Turkish bath**, in a male-free zone in the chocolate factory. The ambience is oriental: baths, massages and rose-perfumed tea (Mariannenstrasse 6, tel: 030 615 14 64, Mon 3–10 pm, Tue–Sun noon–10 pm, variable in summer).

4 Jüdisches Museum

Is it an exploded star of David or simply a metallic zig-zag? This museum of Jewish culture and history designed by Daniel Libeskind created a storm long before it opened in September 2001: even the empty building attracted 350,000 visitors.

At the entrance to the exhibition stands a pomegranate tree made of plastic and silk. That, itself, arouses curiosity, for in Berlin visitors to a Jewish museum might associate such an institution only with the Holocaust. But in Jewish culture the pomegranate tree stands for fertility, and the aim of the Jewish Museum is to illustrate 2,000 years of German-Jewish history.

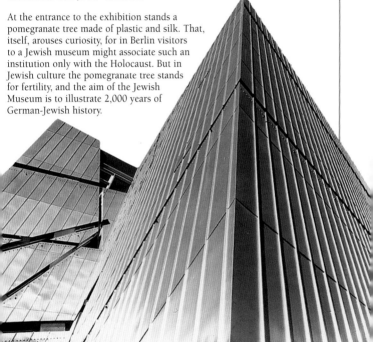

Holocaust Memorial

At first the visitor is left not quite knowing what to expect. The zinc skin of the building reflects the sun. The slits and wedge-shapes in the almost windowless walls could be letters in a secret code. There is no direct entrance; you enter the museum through the building of the baroque law-court which until 1993 housed the Berlin Museum. Walk through the basement into the new building, but you still won't be in the exhibition proper.

The bold shapes of the rooms, the empty ravines and sloping floors are best seen as components of a historical aesthetic: the whole structure is itself a memorial to the Holocaust. The empty spaces, which extend through every floor, are intended to symbolise a vanished culture; the

Light enters the silvery structure through narrow slits

architect calls them "voids". In the high Holocaust-tower, once the door has closed, the visitor is shrouded in darkness and a sense of emptiness prevails. The narrow slits which can be seen from outside promise hope, for they let shafts of light into the building.

A walk through everyday Jewish life

Documents and Biographies

Visitors to the museum learn about German-Jewish history in many and various ways. You can accompany the Hamburg businesswoman Bertha Pappenheim through her life in the 17th century. You can see the briefcase which Gerd W Ehrlich took with him in 1943 when he escaped across the green frontier into Switzerland. His wife gave the briefcase to the museum on permanent loan, as did the many others who contributed their personal mementos. The objects help visitors to understand what life was like for the Jewish community in Germany: books which gave comfort and solace in flight; cutlery which helped to maintain a link with family life.

Displays of photos, coins, weapons and documents lead the visitor through history. You can even look into a contemporary Jewish children's nursery and be surprised to see, from between Hebrew painting books and cassettes, a Barbie doll smiling at you, a smart kippa on her head.

Everything Seems Fine

In the **ETA Hoffmann-Garten**, dwarf oaks grow out of 49 concrete pillars. This stone copse is a memorial to the writer, who sat on the bench of the law-courts in the original building. The slanting pillars in the labyrinth are intended to convey a feeling for the emigrants' life in exile: everything may seem fine, but you don't feel you're standing on firm ground.

TAKING A BREAK

The museum restaurant **Liebermanns** serves refreshments, snacks and Jewish specialities.

➕ 197 D3 ✉ Lindenstrasse 9–14 ☎ (030) 308 78 56 81 🕐 Daily 10–8, except on Jewish feast days (Rosh-Hosanna, Yom Kippur) and 24 Dec 💷 Moderate, children under 6 free; free with *SchauLust* pass (▶ 37) 🚇 Hallesches Tor

---

JÜDISCHES MUSEUM: INSIDE INFO

Top tips Young visitors can follow **children's paths** through the museum, build synagogues and try kosher jelly-babies.
• The **archive of the Leo Baeck Institute**, the most important for German-Jewish history, can be visited by applying in writing (Mon–Thu 10–4; e-mail arcivlbi@jmberlin.de).

5 Bergmannstrasse

The houses and streets in west Kreuzberg are much sought-after film locations. Polish theatrical agents meet Turkish producers in the market hall; people read the *New Yorker* and drink organic red wine – all everyday scenes in Bergmannstrasse.

You could be forgiven for thinking you have been transported back to the end of the 19th century. Historic façades line the street, almost without a gap, between Bergmannstrasse, Heimstrasse and Mehringdamm – a late 19th-century ensemble which it would be hard to match. The nearby Tempelhof airport is the reason: towards the end of World War II, the Allies wanted to keep Tempelhof intact as a landing place for their own planes, it's said, so they didn't bomb the surrounding area.

There are broad streets, ancient trees, lots of shops, bars and theatres, but no empty houses. It's chic to live

In the Beginning

The area around Chamissoplatz has been built up since 1880. Five-storey houses with neo-classical façades arose, but only those with a frontage onto the street were built to a good standard, with bathroom and inside toilet. After World War II the district was neglected for decades. The necessary renovation took 20 years, up to 2001. During this time the rents remained remarkably low.

A Kreuzberg dream: a little shop in Bergmann-strasse

in Bergmannstrasse or Chamissoplatz, so for a long time hardly anyone has wanted to leave. Students who in the 1970s moved into cheap rear-courtyard lodgings may now – as well-paid academics – have decided to buy their renovated apartments and stay.

Marheinekeplatz

On Saturdays dogs bark at the entrance to the market hall in Marheinekeplatz while their owners dawdle at the cheese stall exchanging views on the organic qualities of the wares or passing on the recommendations of the wine critic in the week-end newspaper. In Enoteca (Ludwig-Kirche-Strasse 11) you can try out the real thing – the proprietor claims to be a connoisseur of, especially, Italian wines. The large pots in the square aren't for flowers, they're part of a fountain installation by Paul Pfarr. The Passionskirche at the end of the square is a church only on Sundays; otherwise it's a hall for concerts or discussions.

"Café Achteck"

Chamissoplatz

On the corner of Chamissoplatz, built in the purest classical style of architect Karl Friedrich Schinkel, stands a green "Café Achteck", as the old octagonal public lavatories found all over Berlin are called. The former water tower on the corner of Fidicinstrasse provided the district with water from 1888, then, when it was no longer used to store water, it was lived in until the 1950s, and finally after renovation it became a youth centre and concert hall. At Fidicinstrasse 40, a former metal-ware factory was bought by the artist Kurt Mühlenhaupt in 1991 and converted into an arts centre. The **Friends of Italian Opera** use it, but they don't sing or listen to operas, it's the only English-speaking theatre in the city where international companies perform (tel: (030) 693 56 92).

TAKING A BREAK

Whether it's Swabian, Mexican, Arab or Italian cuisine, everyone can find something to their taste on Bergmannstrasse.

✛ 196 C1 ⊚ Gneisenaustrasse

BERGMANNSTRASSE: INSIDE INFO

Top tips Between Heimstrasse and the Südstern are **four historic cemeteries:** Dreifaltigkeitskirchhof, Friedrichwerderscher Kirchhof, Kirchhof Jerusalems- und Neue Kirchengemeinde, Kirchhof Luisenstadt I. They contain noteworthy monuments, mausoleums and tombs of prominent people (including former chancellor Gustav Stresemann, architect Martin Gropius and artist Adolph Menzel).

• At Mehringdamm 61 is the **Schwules** (Gay) **Museum** (tel: (030) 69 59 90 50, Wed–Mon 2–6, Sat 2–7, U-Bahn station Mehringdamm, admission moderate or free with *SchauLust* pass ► 37).

At Your Leisure

2 Künstlerhaus Bethanien

The vast complex of hospital buildings on Mariannenplatz was built in 1847 to designs by Schinkel's pupil Ludwig Persius as the Bethanien Institute for Deaconesses. When the hospital was shut down in 1970, squatters moved in: 150 young people forced their way into the empty building and named it after Georg von Rauch, a supporter of the RAF (Rote Armee Fraktion – Red Army Group) who was shot dead by a West Berlin policeman. Today, the buildings house several social and cultural organisations.

➕ 198 A3 ✉ Mariannenplatz 2
☎ (030) 616 90 30 🕐 Wed–Sun 2–7
🚇 Görlitzer Bahnhof

6 Viktoriapark

This rambling park is one of the most beautiful in Berlin. From Grossbeerenstrasse the ground rises to the highest spot in the city: 66m (217 feet) above sea level, and from the summit of the hill there are spectacular views across the city. A fairly steep path winds up to the 22m (72-foot) National Memorial with its Iron Cross. Designed by Schinkel in memory of the "Befreiungskrieg" (the 1813–15 campaign which freed the German states from the rule of Napoleon), it gives both hill and district their name (*kreuz* means "cross",

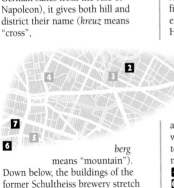

berg means "mountain").

Down below, the buildings of the former Schultheiss brewery stretch

In Riehmers Hofgarten

out; after re-construction they are due to become a town within a town, providing a fine environment for living and working. Hidden in the trees is the Golgatha beer-garden (▶ 152). The park's artificial waterfall will delight young visitors, as will the children's playground.

➕ 196 B1 ✉ Kreuzbergstrasse
🚇 Mehringdamm

7 Riehmers Hofgarten

At Yorckstrasse 83–86, two muscular figures supporting the arch over the entry gate invite visitors into Riehmers Hofgarten, a prime example of an exclusive apartment block from the reign of Wilhelm II (late 19th century). Grouped around landscaped courtyards, linked by an internal road, are 20 four- and five-storey buildings. The apartments were of a generous size when they were built in 1881, and today they contain a quiet hotel in a noisy street.

➕ 196 B1 ✉ Yorckstrasse 83–86
🚇 Mehringdamm

Where to...
Eat and Drink

Prices
Prices are given for one person, excluding drinks.
€ under 12 euros €€ 12–25 euros €€€ over 25 euros

RESTAURANTS

Abendmahl €€
It may be difficult to believe that there is a good restaurant hiding here behind glycinias and a canopy with Chinese lanterns. Despite their unusual names, the dishes on the menu should not be taken as threats – "Flaming Inferno" and "Murder in the Aquarium" turn out to be tasty fish dishes. In spring, daisies decorate your plate. No meat is served.

🕂 198 B3 ⊠ Muskauer Strasse 9
🖀 (030) 612 51 70
🕒 Daily 6 pm–1 am

Coccodrillo €
The chef brings the taste of Mallorca to Kreuzberg. The menu includes tapas, squid kebabs, lamb shank and poultry. As with everywhere at the waterside, the best tables are outside.

🕂 197 F2 ⊠ Am Planufer 92c
🖀 (030) 694 65 18 🕒 Daily
3 pm–1 am

Henne €
Punks and celebs are regular guests at this old Berlin inn, which boasts the crispest milk-fed roast capon.

🕂 197 F3 ⊠ Leuschnerdamm 25
🖀 (030) 614 77 30 🕒 Tue–Sun
from 7 pm

Jolesch €–€€
The room is elegantly old-fashioned with its parquet flooring and chandelier, but the imaginative Austrian cooking is decidedly modern. The cakes are also worth a try.

🕂 198 B3 ⊠ Muskauer Strasse 1
🖀 (030) 612 35 81 🕒 Daily
10 am–1 am, dinner menu from 6 pm

Le Cochon Bourgeois €€
This almost unornamented little bistro, which provides good French country cooking, is to be found in the best area of Kreuzberg.

🕂 197 F1 ⊠ Fichtestrasse 24
🖀 (030) 693 01 01 🕒 Tue–Sat
6 pm–1 am

Max und Moritz €
Sitting on 1918 chairs in this old Berlin inn, you eat Eisbein (knuckle of pork) and Rippenspeer (spare ribs), sometimes accompanied by small art exhibitions and live music.

🕂 197 F3 ⊠ Oranienstrasse 162
🖀 (030) 614 10 45 🕒 Daily
4 pm–1 am

Osteria No 1 €€
Palms and stone flags in the garden, the aroma of garlic, fresh fish, the cries of little children, rapid Italian sentences – the whole is an extraordinarily attractive mix in which to spend a gastronomic summer evening. No wonder the alternative paper tageszeitung was thought up here.

🕂 196 B1 ⊠ Kreuzbergstrasse 71
🖀 (030) 786 91 62 🕒 Daily
noon–2 am

Pagode €
Crowds of people queue for Thai dishes, which you take away from the counter. The selection is large, the cooking good and the portions generous.

🕂 196 C1 ⊠ Bergmannstrasse 88
🖀 (030) 691 26 40 🕒 Daily
noon–midnight

Svevo €€
This unusually elegant restaurant, in a not-at-all-chic area, with minimalist decor (as often happens

Where to... Shop

in Kreuzberg), serves a surprisingly stylish and sophisticated cuisine and has an impressive wine list.

➕ 198 B2 ☒ Lausitzer Strasse 25
☎ (030) 61 07 32 16 ☺ Tue–Sat from 6 pm. Closed Aug

Thymian €–€€

In elegant chic near the Südstern, vegetarians and fish-lovers get their money's worth. Many dishes have an oriental note, thanks to the chef's Turkish roots.

➕ 197 D1 ☒ Gneisenaustrasse 57
☎ (030) 69 81 52 06 ☺ Tue–Sun from 5 pm

Van Loon €–€€

Sitting in a 1918 Dutch sailing barge moored at a jetty in the Landwehrkanal and extended onto a terrace on the bank, you order from a short standard menu with additional seasonal specials.

➕ 197 E2 ☒ Urbanhafen, Carl-Herz-Ufer 5 (near Baerwald bridge)
☎ (030) 692 62 93 ☺ Daily 10 am–1 am

Weltrestaurant Markthalle €–€€

This local institution is for many a kitchen, living-room or work-room. The ambience is traditional, with wood panelling and oak tables, and the cooking is unpretentious.

➕ 198 B3 ☒ Pücklerstrasse 34
☎ (030) 617 55 02 ☺ Daily 9 am–3 am

SNACK BARS

Snack bars in Kreuzberg are cheap and serve dishes from every part of the world.

Abirams

Indian cuisine is served here, in simple surroundings.

➕ 196 C1 ☒ Zossener Strasse 12
☺ Daily noon–midnight

Bica

Enjoy panini (Italian rolls), cakes and coffee in this white-walled Imbiss.

➕ 196 C1 ☒ Chamissoplatz 4
☺ Mon–Fri 9–7, Sat–Sun 10–6

Brooklyn NY

Enormous toasted sandwiches, ice-cream and marshmallows are specialities here.

➕ 197 F3 ☒ Oranienstrasse 176
☺ Mon–Fri 11 am–midnight, Sat–Sun noon–midnight

Curry 36

This is the tops, at least according to Kreuzberg's fans of sausage with curry sauce.

➕ 196 C2 ☒ Mehringdamm 36
☺ Mon–Fri 9 am–4 am, Sat 10 am–4 am, Sun 11 am–3 am

Espresso Bar

Pasta and pizzas are speedily served.

➕ 196 C1 ☒ Mehringdamm 51
☺ Mon–Sat 3 pm–midnight

Seerose

At Seerose vegetarians in a hurry will find an excellent selection. Everything from salad to spinach lasagne is served.

➕ 196 C1 ☒ Mehringdamm 47
☺ Daily 10–10

Anyone walking in the area of Oranienstrasse will notice a host of little specialist shops. Here they are described in order from east to west. Between the Südstern and Mehringdamm there are more odd shops selling interesting things. Explore around Bergmannstrasse and just follow your nose.

AROUND ORANIENSTRASSE

Sterngucker (Spreewaldplatz 4) sells books, toys and gifts. At Zeughofstrasse 21 there is a workshop for old musical instruments, and **Groove Records** (Pücklerstrasse 36) carries the music of independent labels, Ethno and Black Music. **Azienda Agricola Naoiano** (Leuschnerdamm 15) sells excellent olive oil. **Luzifer Now** (Adalbertstrasse 81) has hemp and linen clothing. **Classic Bike-Harley-Davidson Berlin** (Skalitzer Strasse 127–128), sells, hires and repairs the famous bikes and has appropriate accessories. **Alimentari i Vini** (Skalitzer Strasse 23) sells Italian cheeses and sausage, while **suff** (Oranienstrasse 200) offers wine and spirits (Oranienstrasse 200). **Mondlicht** (Oranienstrasse 14) stocks esoteric books, and the women's collective **Kraut und Rüben** (Oranienstrasse 15) sells naturally based cosmetics as well as fruit, vegetables and milk products. **Knof** (Oranienstrasse 185) stocks Mediterranean specialities, **Verrutschi** (Oranienstrasse 180) Kreuzberg fashions, and **DIM** (Oranienstrasse 26) is the outlet for objects made by the Institute for the Blind. **Kisch & Co** (Oranienstrasse 25) sells books, newspapers and

reproduction antiques. **Kalligramm** (Oranienstrasse 28) is a normal antique shop. At **Melek Pastanesi** (Oranienstrasse 28) you can get fresh rolls and oriental sweetmeats 24 hours a day: **Fritz & Fillmann** (Dresdener Strasse 20) stocks an interesting selection of jewellery, **O-ton** (Oranienstrasse 165a) has ceramics, and **Dante Connection** (Oranienstrasse 165) sells works of literature, not only Italian. **Berliner Handpresse** (Prinzessinnenstrasse 20) produces books containing original illustrations.

AROUND BERGMANNSTRASSE

Toys for babies, children and adults are piled up at **Spielbrett** (Körtestrasse 27) and artists' materials are sold at **Jonglerie** (Körtestrasse 26). **kado-authentic flavours** (Graefestrasse 75) promises not only international liquorice specialities but also those of its own make. **Übersee Kontors** (Fichtestrasse 1) has a delicatessen

and wines from southern Europe, Swabia and the Rhineland area and **Broken English** (Grimmstrasse 19) sells British food. **Stabejs Hats** (Grimmstrasse 18) is good for Danish hats and **Reissender Absatz** (Fidicinstrasse 7) specialises in made-to-measure shoes and repairs. **NiK-Noten** in Kreuzberg (Friesenstrasse 7) is a small music shop. In the **market hall** in Marheinekeplatz (Mon–Fri 7:30–7, Sat 7:30–2) you can buy French cheese, German organic bread, Indonesian cigarettes, stockings, jewellery, newspapers and much more. **Fluidum** (Bergmannstrasse 59) stocks artistic water-features; at **UFO** (Bergmannstrasse 25) they sell Sci-Fi, fantasy and horror. At **Hammet** (Friesenstrasse 27) they give very good advice on detective stories, both in the original and in translation. **bagAge** (Bergmannstrasse 13) sells the ultimate in luggage. **Ararat** (Bergmannstrasse 99a) is *the* cult shop for postcards, wrapping paper

and trendy gifts. **Logo** (Bergmannstrasse 10) is a second-hand record shop. **Belladonna** (Bergmannstrasse 101) sells cosmetics based on natural products. **Grober Unfug** (Zossener Strasse 32) is the Eldorado for fans of comics – it has every obtainable German comic, with a wide selection from the USA, France and Great Britain, posters and T-shirts, and it puts on various exhibitions. **Knopf-Paul** (Zossener Strasse 10) has become quite a tourist attraction with its vast selection of buttons, buckles, studs, hooks and eyes... **Das zweite Büro** (Zossener Strasse 6) stocks second-hand office furniture. **Tatau Obscur** (Solmsstrasse 25) does piercing and tattooing. You can buy designer labels at **Molotow** (Gneisenaustrasse 112) and second-hand clothing at **Faster Pussycat** (Mehringdamm 55). **Melitta Sundström** (Mehringdamm 61) combines a gay-lesbian bookshop with a café.

Where to be... Entertained

THEATRE AND MUSIC

Ballhaus Naunynstrasse

(Naunynstrasse 27, tel: (030) 25 88 66 44 for programme information and tickets) is a genuine old Berlin real-tennis court from the 19th century; it's now an arena for experimental dance and music drama, concerts of classical and new-wave music, and a space for international events.

BKA, the Berlin Cabaret Institute high above the roof-tops of Kreuzberg (Mehringdamm 34, tel: (030) 251 01 12), is a famous fringe theatre for every sort of cabaret.

Columbiahalle (Columbiadamm 13–21, tel: (030) 698 09 80) is the place for high-profile events in the city. Formerly there was a gigantic piece of open ground here on the border between Kreuzberg, Tempelhof and Neukölln, with a sports hall and cinema for the US Allies. Now the army has gone it is used for rock, pop and jazz concerts, festivals and techno-parties.

Hebbeltheater (Stresemannstrasse 29, tel: (030) 259 00 40) becomes a mecca for lovers of dance during the annual autumn festival. The art deco theatre is *the* arena for everything experimental, above all in dance, music and performance art.

The castle-like **Passionskirche** (1905–8) often puts on world music and jazz (Marheinekeplatz, tel: (030) 69 40 12 41). Abdullah Ibrahim has appeared here, and so has Ricky Lee Jones.

In 1980 the nurse Irene Moessinger used a legacy to buy a circus tent, which she had erected in Tiergarten with the name of **Tempodrom**. Many well-known performers appeared there. The original tent had to give way to the offices of the Federal Chancellor, but the sensational replacement, a cathedral of high tech, now puts on a varied programme (cabaret, concerts, art shows and major events) behind Anhalter station. If you feel like a swim in a concert hall, you can have one to music in the thermal baths, the **Liquidrom** (Möckernstrasse 10, tel: (030) 611 13 13, swimming Sun–Thu 10–10, Fri–Sat 10 am–midnight, on full-moon nights till 2 am).

Theater am Ufer (Tempelhofer Ufer 10, tel: (030) 251 31 16) is also something special. The Polish proprietor Andrej Woron calls it his "Teatr Kreatur" – a mix of puppet theatre and pantomime, drama and music theatre.

Theater zum Westlichen Stadthirschen (Kreuzbergstrasse 37, tel: (030) 785 70 33), founded in 1982, is one of Kreuzberg's oldest fringe theatres. It shows seldom seen or newly discovered authors' work and puts on unconventional productions of the classics.

CINEMAS

Film-buffs will also find something special in Kreuzberg. **Eiszeitkino** (Zeughofstrasse 20, tel: (030) 611 60 16) shows children's and young people's films, films in the original language, Turkish films, previews, and it has a Beta Film Festival. **fsk** (Segitzdamm 2, on Oranienplatz, tel: (030) 614 24 64, recorded programme listing (030) 61 40 31 95) is equally a paradise for film-buffs, holding premieres and showing many French- and English-language films and documentaries.

BARS

In **Ankerklause** (Kottbusser Damm 104, tel: (030) 693 56 49, Tue–Sun 10 am–4 am, Mon 4 pm–4 am) the best places to sit are on the balcony overlooking the Landwehrkanal, and not only because of the fresh air. The music from the richly stocked jukebox can still be heard out here. Since this local bar was tipped as the place to be it's been invaded by hippy youth.

The tiny **Bierhimmel**, a favourite meeting place for gays and heteros, (Oranienstrasse 183, tel: (030) 615 31 22, daily from 1 pm) is a café during the day, then a bar. Some people even find somewhere to sit, but there's also room to stand, including in the street outside.

Privat Club is in a cellar under the market hall (Pücklerstrasse 34, tel: (030) 611 33 02, Fri–Sat from 11 pm). There's no bouncer at the door; you flop down into the red armchairs and wait to see what's going to happen.

Würgeengel (Dresdener Strasse 122, tel: (030) 615 55 60, daily from 7 pm) takes its name from a film by Luis Buñuel ("The Exterminating Angel") and derives its fame from its cocktails.

Konrad Tönz (Falckenstein-strasse 30, tel: (030) 612 32 52) is a living-room bar named after a character in a TV programme. The programme began at 8:15 pm, and that is when the evening begins here too (Tue–Sun), accompanied by an old record-player.

In **Matto** (Chamissoplatz 4, tel: (030) 691 40 21, daily from 6 pm) beer-drinkers sit at the front, by the large windows, and wine-drinkers at small tables in the back room. *Flammkuchen* (a type of cake from Alsace) a speciality of the house.

The decor of **Wirtschaftswunder** (Yorckstrasse 82, tel: (030) 786 99 99, Sun–Thu 4 pm–4 am, Fri–Sat 4 pm–5 am) evokes the era of the "economic miracle" (late 1940s and 1950s), from which it takes its name. Happy Hour from midnight on – where else do you get that?

Yorckschlösschen (Yorckstrasse 15, tel: (030) 215 80 70, Sun–Thu 9 am–3 am, Fri–Sat 9 am–4 am) also remains steadfastly what it always was, an atmospheric, smoke-filled jazz bar for old Kreuzbergers, with free admission and good solid cooking.

Time has equally stood still in **Junction Bar** (Gneisenaustrasse 18, tel: (030) 694 66 02, daily 8 pm–5 am), where you can listen to live music in the cellar.

Dos Piranhas (Yorckstrasse 81, tel: (030) 785 76 61, Sun–Thu 6 pm–4 am, Fri–Sat 6 pm–6 am) is as good as its name – there are two of the fish looking bored in the aquarium while guests choose from 365 different cocktails and listen to House music.

DANCING

SO 36 (Oranienstrasse 190, tel: (030) 61 40 13 06) has an enticing and varied programme of bingo, karioke, concerts, readings, discos and parties, panel discussions, benefit events and shows. Regulars in their programme include: Café Fatal (tea-dance, Sun 5 pm–1 am), Alles Bingo Bar (every other Tue, 7 pm–1 am), Electric Ballroom (Mon from 11 pm), Hungrige Herzen (gay-lesbian, Wed from 11 pm), Gayhane (gay-lesbian party with Turkish programme, 4th Sat in the month from 10 pm), SahaneHane (Oriental Night House, once a month from 10 pm).

Until 10 pm, **Golgatha**, hidden in Viktoriapark (Dudenstrasse 48–64, tel: (030) 785 24 53, Apr–Oct daily 10 am–6 am), is a beer-garden with trees, a barbecue and cocktail bar. At 10 pm a DJ springs into action, putting anything on that isn't hiphop.

In **WaterGate** (Falckenstein-strasse 49a, tel: (030) 61 28 03 94) the Spree almost laps onto the dance floor while, looming above, the towers of Oberbaumbrücke compete with the Globe logo on the Universal building. Both of WaterGate's two storeys has a bar. On Thursdays it's funk, jazz and soul, on Fridays and Saturdays drum 'n bass and house.

Prenzlauer Berg

Getting Your Bearings

If an urban district could be a myth, then Prenzlauer Berg would be one. Inhabited by actors, writers and painters, critics and rebels, before the fall of the Wall it was the fashionable and intellectual centre of East Berlin. A myth can't be visited, but here you can experience the history of the city almost as if you were in a time-lapse film.

The most important thing first: the district is called Prenzlberg by its traditional inhabitants. The name of the area, which is now an unwilling part of the Pankow district, is derived from the postal address "Prenzl. Berg". Trendy incomers as well as long-time insiders live here; you can hear straight away whether someone belongs or not.

Three-quarters of the residents are newcomers. They have moved into renovated flats or new lofts, and the overwhelming majority are young and well-paid. They appreciate the number of bars and organic markets and the way the designer mile is developing. More children are born here than anywhere else in Berlin.

Before the fall of the Wall the quarter owed its reputation to the decay of the former working-class (blue-collar) district; the resulting cheap apartments opened up opportunities for people to pursue individual lifestyles. The kindergartens and bookshops round Kollwitzplatz are now more or less elegant restaurants. The bronze statue in the children's playground is of a sculptress whose husband was a doctor working among the poor (▶ 159).

In the GDR era Husemannstrasse was already being renovated as a sign of things to come – or half of it was. The street's restored late 19th-century façades are a showcase for a prosperity which never in fact existed before the Wall fell. All the bright and beautiful things are new. Sometimes just five minutes' walk is enough to reveal the old, grey Prenzlberg.

Past times preserved

Page 153: The café mile around Kollwitzplatz

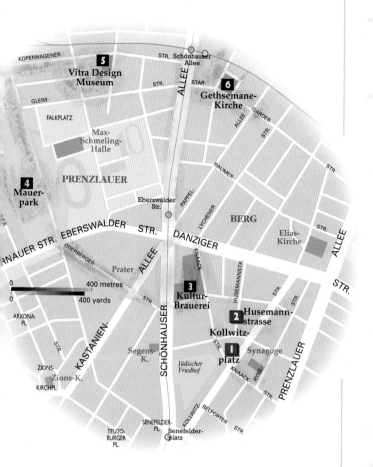

★ Don't Miss

1 Kollwitzplatz ➤ 158

2 Husemannstrasse ➤ 160

At Your Leisure

3 KulturBrauerei ➤ 162

4 Mauerpark ➤ 162

5 Vitra Design Museum ➤ 163

6 Gethsemane-Kirche ➤ 163

Which kind of potatoes was I supposed to bring?

On 9 November, 1989, the whole world saw pictures of the break in the Wall on Bornholmer Strasse. Since then practically everything has changed in Prenzlauer Berg. A decayed artists' quarter has become a trendy district.

Prenzlauer Berg in a Day

10:00 am

You're spoilt for choice with the cafés round ❶ **Kollwitzplatz** (➤ 158–9). If you order your morning coffee at Anita Wronski's (➤ 165), then you're the customer of a Berlin institution. The cafés' terraces overlap each other, but many don't open until later. Only at weekends do people gather here from 10 am for brunch.

11:30 am

Just around the corner, in Rykestrasse, there's a synagogue in the courtyard of one of the houses. The close proximity of the surrounding houses saved it from fire in 1938 (➤ 159). The ground floor is occupied by row upon row of shops selling chic lamps, gifts, Indonesian furniture and beautiful flower arrangements.

12:30 pm

Crossing ❷ **Husemannstrasse** (➤ 160–1), which looks as though it has been well maintained for 100 years, turn left into Sredzkistrasse and then right into Knaackstrasse for the ❸ **KulturBrauerei** (right; ➤ 162). The inscriptions on the restored buildings of this cultural centre inform you that this was once a brewery.

1:30 pm

Leave the brewery by the Schönhauser Allee exit and turn left into Kastanienallee, where you can relax in the Prater restaurant (► 164) – in summer it even has a beer-garden.

3:00 pm

Oderberger Strasse still looks a bit like a dead end, but in fact it leads to **4 Mauerpark** (above; ► 162–3) with its recently planted trees and a brightly painted wall, which separates the park from the sports ground. A former electricity transformer station in Kopenhagener Strasse now houses the **5 Vitra Design Museum** (► 163).

6:00 pm

On the other side of Schönhauser Allee, in Stargarder Strasse, is **6 Gethsemane-Kirche** (► 163), a meeting place for those who, before the fall of the Wall, wanted to see a different GDR and made no secret of their desire for reform.

7:00 pm

Two stops down the U-Bahn and you're almost back to Kollwitzplatz for supper, perhaps in Restauration 1900 (► 165). In summer, you could then take a bottle of wine into Mauerpark and enjoy the daily open-air concert.

❶ Kollwitzplatz

Perhaps it's the architectural unity which makes the square so attractive to residents, workers and visitors alike. It doesn't take much sunshine to entice people out of the surrounding houses onto the café terraces. Kollwitzplatz is the heart of Prenzlauer Berg.

An Island of Culture

During the GDR years, anyone who had the means to do so left the decrepit houses in this densely populated working-class (blue-collar) area and moved into modern concrete-faced blocks of apartments. As they moved out, young people from all parts of the GDR moved in, turning the empty buildings into squats. Gradually an alternative cultural scene evolved in Prenzlauer Berg, with private concerts and readings in apartments and rear courtyards. Actors, painters, song-writers and students, sympathetic to the peace movement in the West, felt at home here.

At midnight on 2/3 October, 1990, in Café Westphal, the "Autonome Republik Utopia" (Autonomous Republic of Utopia) was declared. It was, according to the founding declaration, "to become a home for all those who look reality in the eye and nevertheless refuse to give up hope for the future of humanity". The new citizenship was christened with kirsch-whisky, a GDR invention.

Café Westphal no longer exists. Yesterday's tatty chic has been ousted by western firms on behalf of financially powerful clients. The surrounding shops sell things to beautify the home. Greatly increased rents have driven the sculptors, painters and photographers out of their studios.

No other district has Prenzlauer Berg's birthrate

Local Girl

Not until 1947 was the former Wörther Platz renamed in honour of the sculptress and illustrator Käthe Kollwitz. Her husband Karl Kollwitz was a doctor working among the poor, and from 1892 to 1943 she lived with him in a house on the corner of Knaackstrasse. This is where she found her inspiration. Kaiser Wilhelm II was publicly abusive about her work. The Nazis forced her out of her posts in the Prussian Academy of Arts. In 1943 her house was bombed and the couple moved to Moritzburg near Dresden, where she died.

If you look up, you'll see greenery sprouting from the new roof-terraces. In the playground, children climb around, as they have since 1959, on the memorial to Käthe Kollwitz (1867–1945). Gustav Seitz based his bronze of the sculptress (➤ panel above) on a self-portrait from 1938.

The four-storey brick-built house at Rykestrasse 53 has a **synagogue** in its rear courtyard. Only fear of the blaze spreading to the neighbouring houses saved the synagogue on "Kristallnacht" (9 November, 1938), when so many other synagogues in Berlin were burnt down; instead it was used as a stable. After restoration in 1953 the building was re-consecrated and is now Germany's largest synagogue.

The **water tower** on Windmühlenberg is the icon of the district. In the 18th and 19th centuries dozens of windmills were operating here. Construction of the water tower began in 1855; it was the first in Berlin. It went into operation in 1877 but was shut down in 1952 and is now just a private house. In the Nazi era the cellar was a notorious torture-chamber.

The Jewish cemetery

TAKING A BREAK

There's no shortage of places to sit, eat and drink in and around Kollwitzplatz. You can choose whichever place appeals most to you – there is no great difference between the various cafés.

➕ 193 F5 🚇 Senefelder Platz

KOLLWITZPLATZ: INSIDE INFO

Top tips The **Ayurveda-Centre Surya Villa** has elephants in its courtyard and colonial-style furniture; it offers holistic massage and steam baths for the elimination of toxins (courtyard of Rykestrasse 9, diagonally opposite the synagogue, tel: (030) 48 49 57 89).

• The **Jewish cemetery**, consecrated in 1827, contains the tombs of the composer Giacomo Meyerbeer, the painter Max Liebermann and Bismarck's financial adviser Gerson von Bleichröder (Schönhauser Allee 23–25, Mon–Thu 8–4, Fri 8–1).

❷ Husemannstrasse

The GDR had in mind an exemplary total renovation when it reconstructed Husemannstrasse as part of the city's 750th anniversary celebrations. It made a good beginning.

Stroll down Husemannstrasse today and you'll find cafés and small boutiques lining the street. Short flights of steps lead down into the basements of the former tennements and notices in Gothic script announce what's on offer on the ground floor. Usually, you'll find it's curios or junk, but take a glance through the window of many a renovated house façade and you may well discover that a Thai, Irish or Chinese restaurant has moved in.

In 1984 legions of building workers arrived in Kollwitzplatz to smarten up the run-down 19th-century buildings for the jubilee of the capital of the GDR. By 1987, they had brought 24 façades, as far as Sredzkistrasse, up to the standard expected of the locality.

The Forerunner of Prefabrication

The reason for the – admittedly pretty – uniformity of the street is that the firm that built it in 1890 (Deutsch-Holländische Actienverein) was the first to use standardised features: ornamentation of the façades, balustrades and ceiling joists. That made it all faster and cheaper. The bricks were made just round the corner, in Helmholtzplatz.

Forgotten Resistence?

Walter Husemann was a young communist from Pankow. He was 33 years old when he was murdered in Plötzensee in 1943 for opposing Hitler's regime. Ernst Knaack and Siegmund Sredzki, who also have local streets named after them, suffered the same fate.

Husemann-strasse in 1990

Meteoric

Around 1830, 300 people lived in the area of Prenzlauer Berg. By 1930, there were 326,000 inhabitants, making it the most densely populated district in Berlin. Industrialisation attracted workers to the factories in the city and caused great housing shortages. Behind the beautiful façades more and more grim blocks were built, round courtyards that grew ever smaller, down to the minimum allowed dimension of 17 square feet – the space which a fire-engine needed to turn. After the war the quarter gradually decayed.

A Faithful Copy of the Past

Here the lanterns are made from cast iron, the street signs look old, and guild signs shine with gold. The inscriptions on shop-fronts and work-shops are also faithful copies, making the street into something of a living museum: "made-to-order" firms and dressmakers' shops offer their services.

Shortly after the fall of the Wall someone did in fact set up a hackney carriage (taxi) and charabanc (bus) company with its own stop just across the road. In 1989, under the auspices of the "Genossenschaft der Berliner Figaros, Hundepfleger und Kosmetiker" (Association of Berlin Barbers, Dog-groomers and Beauticians), a hairdressing museum exhibited comical things like moustache-covers and spittoons from the Charlie Chaplin era. There was also a "Museum des Berliner Arbeiterlebens um 1900" (Museum of German Workers' Lives around 1900). Few were interested in any of this, and now they're all history as well.

Few inns have been so immune to the change of regime as Restauration 1900

TAKING A BREAK

Restauration 1900 (Husemannstrasse 1; ➤ 165) has kept its pleasant atmosphere unchanged since 1986.

➕ 193 F5 　🚇 Eberswalder Strasse

HUSEMANNSTRASSE: INSIDE INFO

Top tip Furniture (Sredzkistrasse 22), with its eerily beautiful patterns, is itself a sort of design museum of the 1960s.

At Your Leisure

❸ KulturBrauerei

The brewery site between Schönhauser Allee and Knaackstrasse, originally the headquarters of the Schultheiss brewery, is a city within a city. Covering an area of 2.5ha (6 acres), it was built between 1890 and 1910 to plans by Franz Schwechten, the head of the royal planning department and

Once a fortress of beer, now of culture

architect of the Kaiser-Wilhelm-Gedächtniskirche (➤ 118). The brewery continued to operate in this brick fortress until 1965, although for the final 20 years only the bottling was done at Knaackstrasse. The names of the various sections are written over doors and gateways: *Heuboden* (hayloft), *Sattlerei* (saddlery), *Flaschenbier* (bottled beer) and *Böttcherwerkstatt* (cooperage), *Stellmacherei* (cartwrights' workshop) and

Schlosserei (metalworking shop). It's amazing what a lot went on in a brewery which was just one of many in Prenzlauer Berg.

Nowadays not a drop of beer is brewed in the district. Culture has moved into the buildings, all of which are listed. Renamed KulturBrauerei, the Schultheiss brewery quickly became famous after the fall of the Wall. The place where East Berlin rockers in leather gear once took over the old canteen was now to be a home for fringe culture. Private TV stations arrived, attracted by the idea of the "threadbare space" as a backdrop. Studios, workshops and a concert hall sprang into being. After renovation, a puppet theatre, a cinema and a beer-hall moved in. The first cultural wave seems quietly to have moved out, and those people now meet a few yards further on, at Prater (➤ 164) in Kastanienallee, a place that is still untouched by the passage of time.

🔢 193 F5 🖂 Knaackstrasse 75–97/ Schönhauser Allee 36–39 ☎ (030) 441 92 70 🚇 Eberswalder Strasse

❹ Mauerpark

Oderberger Strasse was for a long time one of the most neglected streets round Kollwitzplatz. After the Wall was removed it too obviously led nowhere. Blackened by time, the Stadtbad (city baths; No 57–59) sit there gloomily like a deserted little castle, coming fleetingly to life when occasional readings are held in it. Since 2000 the Mauerpark (Wall Park) has been developed at the end of the street, on the site of the former station goods yard, through which the Wall had run since 1961. Variously planted, and broken up with lawns and open spaces, it is bounded by a graffiti wall leading down to Jahn stadium. An ecological garden and children's farm were planned, to bring

a church nave; here international touring exhibitions are arranged on topics like design, fashion, advertising and architecture.

➕ 193, north-bound E5
✉ Kopenhagener Strasse 58 ☎ (030) 473 77 70 🕐 Tue–Sun 11–8, Fri 11–10 🚇 Schönhauser Allee
💷 Expensive

6 Gethsemane-Kirche

In autumn 1989 this evangelical church became known far beyond the parish boundaries. For Berlin it was the meeting-place of the opposition to the regime. Built in 1893, the church is one of the biggest places of worship in the city, well suited to large assemblies.

In the weeks before the fall of the Wall, civil rights broadsheets were posted up on the walls, services of exhortation were held and prayers for intercession were said. Song writers and singers who were forbidden from performing elsewhere found an audience here. In front of the entrance candles were lit, to show everyone the way – eventually great mountains of wax built up. On the evening of 7 October, 1989, a brutal police action put an end to the meetings. Here too, a month later, on 9 November, the first break was made in the Wall, at Bornholmer Strasse.

➕ 193, north-bound F5
✉ Stargarder Strasse
🚇 Schönhauser Allee

The meeting-place of the GDR opposition: Gethsemane-Kirche

more greenery to the area, but anyway dogs are glad to have space to romp around in.

On long summer evenings, concerts bring back memories of Woodstock, and during the "Winter Olympics for Dolls and Soft Toys" teddy bears rush across Behmstrasse bridge away from the former no-man's-land.

➕ 193 D5 🚇 Eberswalder Strasse

3 Vitra Design Museum

The brick building looks distinctly well fortified. It used to be an electricity transformer station before becoming an offshoot of the famous Designmuseum in Weil am Rhein (built in 1989 by Frank Gehry) and an exhibition centre for an extensive collection of various kinds of seating. The industrial memorial occupying the former machine hall has the dimensions of

Where to...
Eat and Drink

Prices

Prices given are for one person, excluding drinks.

€ under 12 euros €€ 12–25 euros €€€ over 25 euros

RESTAURANTS

K Fröhlich €

A long time ago Herr Kalle Fröhlich is said to have opened a grocer's shop in an area which even today is way off the tourist routes. Later a Michelin-starred chef from Bavaria moved into the building, opposite the Drama School's theatre. He procured the necessary paraphernalia, rough late 19th-century wooden tables and chairs, and now prepares what used in 1871 to be called an economical cuisine, but which he calls regional. Its regional for the typical new

Berliner – for example, there's Bavarian *Spätzle* (noodles), Viennese *schnitzel* and Italian lasagne, but also liver with pears, cabbage stew or Sunday roasts.

✚ 193 F4 ✉ Belforter Strasse 22 ☎ (030) 41 72 52 42 ⊙ Mon–Sat from noon, Sun from 10 am 🚫 No credit cards

OKI €€

This is a small experimental restaurant with a Japanese flavour. The programme – that is, the menu – is exhibited on the wall on a sort of broadsheet. The large rolls of paper inform you that the cooking

is North German-Japanese: fish and joints of meat baked whole and served with rice and vegetables from the wok. There's no lack of variations on *sushi* and *sashimi*, with or without salad. The fish soup is reminiscent of jasmine tea. The chef also makes great pastries, served as dessert or in the afternoon with coffee.

✚ 193 E5 ✉ Oderberger Strasse 23 ☎ (030) 49 85 31 30 ⊙ Tue–Sun 3–11 pm, hot meals from 6:30 🚫 No credit cards

Ostwind €–€€

Years ago a student of German from Beijing decided to start cooking, Chinese-style of course, but without the usual taste-enhancer MSG (monosodium glutamate). He also abandoned the usual red-décor, lions and oriental landscapes in favour of simple furnishings, and his venture is a success. Meat and vegetables simmer over a low heat in a cooking-pot from Shanghai, while

the family or friends sit round, eating with chopsticks and talking non-stop.

✚ 193 F5 ✉ Husemannstrasse 13 ☎ (030) 441 59 51 ⊙ Mon–Sat 6 pm–1 am, Sun 10 am–1 am

Prater €

In 1862, way outside the city, there was a popular little beer pub called Café Chantant. When the horse-tram reached the area in 1875, it became an attractive place to live and was soon built up. In 1880 the pub added a theatre, concert hall and buffet room and adopted its present name. Berliners came with the whole family to spend their leisure time here – it was just the place for the rousing speeches of the workers' leaders. Rosa Luxemburg spoke here, as did August Bebel. In 1960 an open-air theatre was constructed in the garden, and on Sundays the local cultural centre put on dances. It all came to an end in 1991, but when an offshoot of the Volksbühne

(➤ 45) moved here the inn and beer-garden revived. You sit at simple old tables and chairs and order good plain cooking. In the beer-garden it's self-service.

⊞ 193 E5 ⊠ Kastanienallee 7–9 ☎ (030) 448 56 88 ⓦ Inn: Mon–Sat from 6 pm, Sun from 10 am. Garden: Mon–Fri from 4 pm, Sat–Sun from noon, Apr–Sep ⓦ No credit cards

Restauration 1900 €€

The name is an exaggeration, ever though you wouldn't guess it from the furnishings. This institution has been watching over Kollwitzplatz only since 1986, during which time it has seen many things come and go. For some time it was the only restaurant worthy of the name in the square. The breakfast is generous, regional specialities are on offer, but the lamb is unambiguously Provençal. It's worth a visit at any time of day.

⊞ 193 F5 ⊠ Husemannstrasse 1 ☎ (030) 442 24 94 ⓦ Daily from 10 am

Weinstein €€

The name says it all: 500 sorts of wine are the main attraction to the clientele of this extremely friendly place. A short but substantial menu is written up on a board and rubbed off again the next day to make way for other dishes using fresh ingredients.

⊞ 193, north-bound F5 ⊠ Lychener Strasse 33 ☎ (030) 441 18 42 ⓦ Mon– Sat 5 pm–2 am, Sun 6 pm–2 am

SNACK BARS

Konnopke

This establishment has been well known since 1930, but became famous since the fall of the Wall. Max Konnopke sold *Kartoffelpuffer* (potato fritters), fish fillets and sausages in two shifts from half past four in the morning till half past six in the evening. His granddaughter Waltraud Ziervogel is the third-generation fryer, especially of the Berlin favourite: sausages with curry sauce. *"Ohne oder mit?"* (With or without?) is the question you'll be asked. "Without" (skin) is the popular choice, and the recipe for the sauce is naturally a family secret. Hungry early risers can usually be rewarded with Konnopke's tasty "peasant" omelette.

⊞ 193, north-bound E5 ⊠ Schönhauser Allee 44a/Unter der Hochbahn ⓦ Mon–Fri 6 am–8 pm

New York Sandwich

Twenty-three varieties of this American snack are on offer, hot or cold, with or without salad, as well as American-style muffins and American beer.

⊞ 193, north-bound E5 ⊠ Schönhauser Allee 65 ⓦ Mon–Fri 8–8, Sat 9–7, Sun 11–5

CAFÉS

Anita Wronski

This café on Kollwitzplatz has won many faithful friends with its famously large, inexpensive breakfast. But it's worth a visit after 4 pm as well.

⊞ 193 F5 ⊠ Knaackstrasse 26 ☎ (030) 442 84 83 ⓦ Daily 9 am– 2 am, breakfast Mon–Fri until 4 pm, Sat–Sun buffet 10 am–3 pm

Immu

It may be small, but Immu serves breakfast all day, including juicy fruit tarts. Late risers get their money's worth.

⊞ 193, north-bound F5 ⊠ Lychener Strasse 41 ☎ (030) 44 71 66 98 ⓦ Daily 8 am–midnight

Pasternak

Once you've deciphered the Cyrillic script you get the idea: Russian favourites are the main things served here. Caviar, pancakes with *quark* (curd cheese) and *solyanka* (spicy ragout) are on the menu, and it's always breakfast time. There is often live Russian folk music.

⊞ 193 F5 ⊠ Knaackstrasse 22 ☎ (030) 442 88 07 ⓦ Daily 9 am–2 am

Where to... Shop

Arrive after midday, or still better after 2 pm and before 7 pm, otherwise you may find a notice on the door "*Ich bin gleich wieder da*" (Back soon). It's a good idea to try the door all the same – some of these notices are probably never taken down.

Thatchers (Kastanienallee 21) sells avant-garde ladies' fashions, **mutabilis** (Stubbenkammerstrasse 4) conjures sexy clothing out of boring bits and pieces (fasteners, stand-up collars, rubberised materials), and the fashion designer **Mane Lange** (Hagenauer Strasse 13) creates corsets out of velvet, silk, brocade and lace. Many of the goods in **LederArt** (Wörther Strasse 26) come from the

designer's own collection. You can get clubbing gear at **Blue Moon** (Danziger Strasse 26) or **Eisdieler** (Kastanienallee 12). If you want to take a step back in time, go to **The Black Rose** (Danziger Strasse 25), where you'll find retro clothes.

Black Dog (Rodenbergstrasse 9) sells nothing but American comics. **Antiquariat Güntheroth** (Schönhauser Allee 20) stocks old GDR editions, well sorted and inexpensive, and the children's bookshop **Le Matou** (Husemannstrasse 29) has books for children and teenagers in 18 different languages.

VoPo Records (Danziger Strasse 31) is a cult address with a wide range of music: hiphop, indie, hardcore and punk, but also country and surf. **Strandgut** (Oderberger Strasse 4) sells new and second-hand soul and boogie. You can get everything for Goa parties, from trance music on CD and vinyl to the right outfit, at **triballtools** (Lychener Strasse 10).

Where to be... Entertained

NIGHT-LIFE

At **Koi Klub Mangas** (2nd Wed in the month) and at **Open Leinwand** events you can watch films in the **8-mm Bar** (Schönhauser Allee 177b, tel: (030) 40 50 06 24, Mon–Sat 9 pm –3 am, Sun 8 pm–2 am). **August Fengler** (Lychener Strasse 11, tel: (030) 44 35 66 40, daily from 7 pm, programme starts 10 pm, admission free) is the place for Caribbean sounds and Black Music. "Trashy" is the description for **Bastard@Prater**, Kastanienallee 7–9, tel: (030) 44 04 96 69). The walls are covered in old newspaper photos, the drinks menu flickers with "Poetry Slam" are held on the first Thursday in the month, starting at 10 pm, while for the

Karrera Club (indie-pop, rock, brit-pop, punk rock) doors open at 11 pm on the first Saturday in the month. The former GDR youth club **Duncker** (Dunckerstrasse 64, tel: (030) 445 95 09, Mon, Tue, Thu, Sun from 10 pm, Fri, Sat from 11 pm) has hippy-shake music every Tuesday. Neon lighting leads to **Geburtstags-Klub** (Am Friedrichshain 33, Mon, Fri, Sat from 11 pm), for reggae; on the third Saturday in the month they put on "Irrenhaus" (madhouse), with house and disco. Fabulous drum 'n' bass nights are at designer cellar **Icon** (Cantianstrasse 15, tel: (030) 61 28 75 45, Fri–Sat from 11:30 pm).

The boiler house in **KulturBrauerei** (Knaackstrasse 97, tel: (030) 441 92 70, Sun–Thu from 8 pm, Fri–Sat from 9 pm) has live Russian ska.

Excursions

All three destinations are linked by the romantic image of the legendary "Mark Brandenburg sands". For many centuries, these natural or man-made idylls were among the most favoured retreats for royalty and long ago became popular destinations for trips out of the city.

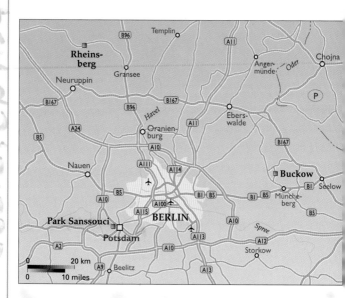

Potsdam: Sanssouci

It's just a hop, skip and a jump to the neighbouring city of Potsdam, 30km (18 miles) west of central Berlin. The gardens and palaces of Park Sanssouci, first laid out in the 18th century by Friedrich II (Frederick the Great), are the main attractions here and it is rare for a visitor to Berlin to miss this idyll on the River Havel.

Schloss Sanssouci

Just four years after his accession in 1740, Friedrich II began work on a summer retreat west of Potsdam, replacing a more modest residence established by his father. He named it Schloss Sanssouci (the name means "free of care" in French) and set about creating landscape gardens in the surrounding parkland. Park Sanssouci is vast, covering an area of 300ha (740 acres). Peter Joseph Lenné created one of his most beautiful landscape gardens here. After just a few steps into the grounds, the view opens out on several axes to reveal the castle, the later Neues Palais, a windmill, a fountain and a ruin. Lenné called these axes the "facial lines".

Star in Park Sanssouci

It is best to approach Schloss Sanssouci through the wrought iron **Grüne Gitter** (Green Gate) in the **Marlygarten**. Friedrich Wilhelm I, Friedrich II's father, had a vegetable garden planted here, which he ironically called his "Marly" – the name of the generous gardens belonging to the French king Louis XIV. This was replaced in the 19th century by the formal garden that exists today.

Friedrich designed **Schloss Sanssouci** himself and between 1745 and 1747 Georg Wenzeslaus von Knobelsdorff, the most prominent north German architect of his time, turned his plans into reality. The palace was built above six vineyard terraces, with a wide flight of 132 steps leading up to it. From the base of the steps, the palace's copper dome, bearing the distinctive blue-green patina of age, is only just visible, seeming almost to float between the vines and the sky. Statues, wreathed in vines, shoulder the serene rococo palace. The 12 rooms are elaborately decorated with gilded carving, relief work and paintings, mirrors and inlaid floors.

**Page 167:
A long climb leads to Schloss Sanssouci**

Prussian Arcadia

Art historians have puzzled over why Friedrich built a summer palace that was so small and impractical, and for its time so unpretentious; after all, he wasn't as miserly as his father, the Soldier King (► 23). Perhaps there is a clue in the picture above the door in the concert room: a vineyard with a castle above the bank of a river and in front boats, sheep and a gravestone inscribed "*Et in Arcadia ego*".

Tea ceremony under the golden palms of the Chinesisches Teehaus (► 170)

The king certainly loved is summer palace and wanted to be buried here, although his wishes were not followed when he died. In 1991, his remains were transferred from

Hohenzollern Castle, and he was given an elaborate state funeral which he had never wanted. It was his fifth.

Around Park Sanssouci

Close to Schloss Sanssouci, you'll find **Friedenskirche** (Church of Peace; 1845–54). The church was designed by Persius as a columned basilica with campanile and cloister.

Pure showing off – the Neues Palais

The **Bildergalerie** (Picture Gallery; 1755–63), also nearby, is typical of the baroque era. It is virtually covered with historical paintings from the Renaissance and baroque periods, and ranks as one of the oldest art museums in Europe.

The **Neue Orangerie** (New Orangery; 1851–61) is reminiscent of Italian Renaissance villas. It was built as a guest-house for Tsar Nicholas and his wife, Friedrich Wilhelm IV's sister. Tropical and sub-tropical plants thrive in the greenhouses of the Botanic Gardens below the Orangery.

From the upper terrace of the Orangery the path leads to the **Drachenhaus** (Dragon House; 1770–2), designed by Gontard in the Chinese look popular at that time. This was the home of the wine grower who looked after the vineyard. The **Chinesisches Teehaus** (Chinese Teahouse; 1754–6) on the other side of the Maulbeerallee serves purely as decoration. Its floor plan is in the shape of a cloverleaf, gilded palms support the portico and gleaming golden life-sized figures enjoy a tea ceremony accompanied by music. Inside, 18th-century porcelain is on display.

In the eyes of the public the 240m (262-yard) long, three-winged and bombastically adorned **Neues Palais** (New Palace) takes second place to Schloss Sanssouci. Through it Friedrich wished to demonstrate Prussian power following the Seven Years War (1756–63). Around 400 sculptures clutter the palace, crammed full of marble and shells – a "fanfare", pure showing off, Friedrich himself called it.

Even when you have seen all that, you still have the extensive greenery, the bubbling fountains, the smiling cherubs, the chirping of the birds to enjoy.

✉ Schloss Sanssouci ☎ (0331) 969 41 90 🕐 Schloss Sanssouci: Tue–Sun 9–5, Apr–Oct; Tue–Sun 9–4 (with tour only), rest of year. Damenflügel (Ladies' Wing) in Palace: Sat, Sun 10–5, 15 May–15 Oct. Picture Gallery: Tue–Sun 10–5, 15 May–15 Oct; New Chambers: Tue–Sun 10–5, 15 May–15 Oct; Sat–Sun 10–5, 1 Apr–14 May. Historic Windmill: Daily 10–6, Apr–Oct; 10–5, rest of year. Orangery: Tue–Sun 10–5, 15 May–15 Oct. Chinese Teahouse: Tue–Sun 10–5, 15 May–15 Oct. Church of Peace: Daily 10–6, May–Oct. New Palace: Sat–Thu 9–5, Apr–Oct; Sat–Thu 9–4, rest of year. Schloss Charlottenhof: Tue–Sun 10–12:30, 1–5 (with tour only), 15 May–15 Oct. Roman Baths: Tue–Sun 10–12:30, 1–5, 15 May–15 Oct. 🚉 Potsdam Main Station 🚌 695 or Tram 96 💲 Expensive

Rheinsberg

The castle, park, charming town and surrounding lakes combine to make Rheinsberg a popular excursion from Berlin. The town is renowned for its connections with Friedrich II (Frederick the Great) and the writer Kurt Tucholsky.

A statue of a youthful Friedrich II genially greets visitors to **Schloss Rheinsberg**. "Young Fritz" was given the castle on the shores of Grienericksee (Lake Grienerick) by his father and lived happily here for four years, from 1736 to 1740, before being summoned to Berlin as king. During this time, he extended the palace and decorated it in rococo style. As king, he remembered his time at Rheinsberg with great fondness.

His flamboyant younger brother, Prince Heinrich, then became lord of the castle, remaining so for over 60 years until his death in 1802. He is buried in the pyramid tomb that he had erected.

In 1912, Kurt Tucholksy wrote the tenderly playful *Ein Bilderbuch für Verliebte (Picture Book for Lovers)*. His love story, which was set in Rheinsberg, became a bestseller, bringing the lake and castle literary fame and a stream of visitors that continues to this day. A memorial to Tucholsky has been erected in the castle.

Schloss Rheinsberg
☎ (033931) 72 60 🕐 Tue–Sun 9:30–12:30, 1–5, Apr–Oct; Sat–Sun 10–12:30, 1–4, rest of year 💶 Moderate

Tucholsky-Gedenkstätte (Tucholsky Memorial)
☎ (033931) 390 07 🕐 Tue–Sun 9:30–12:30, 1–5 💶 Inexpensive

Directions: 85km (53 miles) northwest of Berlin; A24, exit Neuruppin, or B96 to Gransee, then secondary roads; regional train connection from Berlin

Friedrich II and his brother Heinrich both lived in the castle at Rheinsberg

Buckow

National Park Märkische Schweiz is the name of the landscape of hills and lakes to the east of Berlin, which attracted writers and is still today one of the most popular destinations for city dwellers.

The centre and thus the pearl of the Märkische Schweiz lies on the bank of Schermützelsee (Lake Schermützel) and is called Buckow. Citizens of Berlin had villas built here at the end of the 19th century, and those from East Berlin visited their weekend cottages in Buckow during the GDR era. Many writers contributed to the reputation of the area. Chamisso as well as Fontane knew how to describe it sensitively. Still remaining is Bertolt Brecht's summer residence from 1952 to 1956, "a not inelegantly built cottage", as he described it in his work journal. Since 1977 it has been a memorial. Entry is via a high, well-lit salon with a heavy wooden table, and with trunks and benches from the 18th and 19th centuries.

"A not inelegantly built cottage"

Underfoot the black-stained floorboards in front of the chimney creak. In summer readings or musical entertainment sometimes take place. Brecht is said to have preferred to work outside in the boathouse, where today the covered wagon stands. In 1949 the wagon pulled Brecht's wife Helene Weigel as Mother Courage for the first time across the stage of the Berlin Ensemble. A stone balustrade separates garden and lake. Copper plaques display poems from the famous Buckow Elegies which originated here in 1953.

A memento to Mother Courage, Helene Weigel

Brecht-Weigel-Haus
✉ Bertolt-Brecht-Strasse 30 ☎ (033433) 467 🕐 Daily 1–6, Apr–Oct; Mon–Fri 10–12, 1–4, Sat, Sun 11–4, rest of year 💶 Moderate

Directions: 60km (37 miles) east of Berlin; B1, Train Müncheberg, Bus 928

Walks & Tours

1 SPANDAU TO POTSDAM

By boat

Those who don't take a ride on the steamer when in Berlin don't really get to know the city. From the water it doesn't appear stony and industrial. It becomes leisurely, at times idyllic and even rural.

DISTANCE: 17km (10 miles) **TIME:** 2 hours
START POINT: Spandau Lindenufer (Stern und Kreis Schiffahrt) ☎ (030) 53 63 600, Easter to September) 🚇 Rathaus Spandau **END POINT:** Potsdam

1–2

The trip begins on Lindenufer, on the outskirts of the attractive Spandauer Altstadt (old centre of Spandau). Spandau has officially been part of Berlin since 1920 but its low-set houses in an expansive pedestrian zone give it a provincial town atmosphere. The 15th-century **Gothisches Haus** (Gothic House), once a merchant's residence, represents the oldest preserved residential building in Berlin. And in the **St Nikolaikirche** (Church of St Nicholas), Elector Joachim II sealed the end of Catholicism and introduced Lutheran teaching into the Mark. Where the passenger ships to Wannsee and Potsdam depart today, were once the wall and ramparts of the town fortifications. A fraction further north

between industrial sites, the Spree flows quietly into the Havel and hitches a ride with it to the south.

2–3

At first the boat passes to what is clearly the rear of Spandau – the water was a place of work, not residence – then to the left the Südhafen (southern harbour) can be seen. Like an idyllic village the former fishing port **Tiefwerder** lies on

the Unterhafen (lower harbour), a mixture of shipyard and boathouses, clubs and blocks of apartments. Tiny garden plots with caravans or small summerhouses stand side by side on 5m (16-foot) wide branches of the river. After the bridge, over which the Heerstrasse runs, a historical village tavern nestles in on the right among the monstrous residential blocks of the 1960s. Boats of various sizes bob in enormous marinas. It is hard to believe that in September 1816 the first steamship built in Europe, the *Prinzessin Charlotte von Preussen* (Princess Charlotte of Prussia), was launched.

3–4

Pichelswerder on the left was a wood trading centre in the 18th century and has been a popular destination for

SPANDAU

Havel • Lindenufer • Spree
Stresow
Spandau ★ 1
Süd-
hafen
Scharfe HEERSTR. • Pichelsberg • Olympia-
stadion
2 Lanke
Tiefwerder
Weinmeister-
horn • 3 Pichels-
werder
4
Schildhorn
Villa Lemm • Havel • Grunewaldturm

two centuries. Its pubs were once famous. The area was taken over long ago by water-sports clubs, and on fine weekends it is as busy here as on the Kudamm (▶114) in central Berlin. The Havel becomes wider, its branches flow together and looking back, one can see Scharfe Lanke on the right, the most famous of the Spandau bays with its particularly chic boats. These expensive moorings are also quickly and easily accessible via the Heerstrasse. In the conspicuous dive tower on the DLRG premises, lifesavers can practise in deep water.

repaired large inland ships. Today on this site there are services for water travellers and a boat petrol station. On the **Schildhorn**, the point to the left, Albrecht the Bear defeated the Slavic Prince Jaczo in 1157, according to Berlin legend. Emerging out of the trees on the Karlsberg to the left is the **Grunewaldturm** (Grunewald Tower), a gift from the district of Teltow (south of Berlin) to commemorate the 100th birthday of Kaiser

Tiefwerder: idyll behind the shipyards and residential area

4–5
On the slopes of the Lanke Shipyards marina, at **Weinmeisterhorn** on the right, runs tended vines in the Middle Ages. Berlin's first marina originated here about 35 years ago. The Lanke Shipyards for decades built and

werder

Strandbad
Wannsee

Grosser
Wann-
see

Nikolassee

Wannsee

Wannsee

7

8

Sacrow

Pfauen-
insel

Sacrower See

Volkspark
Klein-Glienicke

Heilands-
kirche

9

Glienicker
Brücke

Havel

POTSDAM

Potsdam 10
jetty

manicured lawns to celebrate the birthday of Her Majesty, Queen Elizabeth II. Today the site belongs to a businessman.

5–6

The attractive **Schwanenwerder** peninsula behind the sailing school and surfers' paradise was praised in the 19th century by French novelist Henri Stendhal as an isle full of charm. After 1933 it was known in Berlin as "Bonzenwerder" ("Bigwig-werder"): Hitler's architect Albert Speer and Joseph Goebbels lived here. The Americans seized the island and it became the residence of Lucius D Clay, the "father of the airlifts".

6–7

The boat passes **Strandbad Wannsee** (Wannsee Beach) and anchors in Wannsee where passengers board and disembark. Barely has the journey begun again, and there is a noticeably cool breeze.

7–8

The next stop is the **Pfaueninsel** (Peacock Island). Those who wish to visit it must transfer to a ferry. The "pearl of the Havel", 98ha (237 acres) in size, became famous as the love nest of the Prussian Elector and

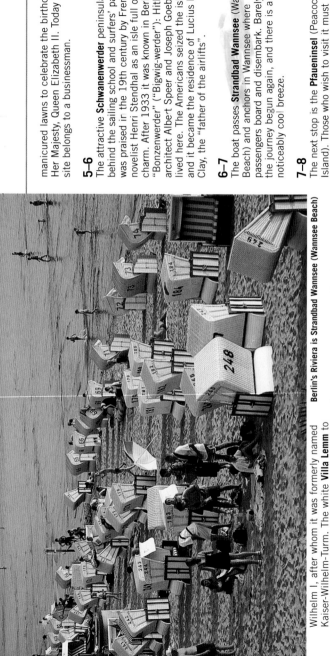

Berlin's Riviera is Strandbad Wannsee (Wannsee Beach)

In June every year, West Berliners keenly looked on as officers with their red jackets and ladies with large hats gathered on the

Wilhelm I, after whom it was formerly named Kaiser-Wilhelm-Turm. The white **Villa Lemm** to the right lies on the Gatow rowing route. Until the beginning of the 1990s this villa was the headquarters of the British military governors.

Taking a Break

For those feeling peckish, snacks and drinks are available on the **boats**.

Glienicker Brücke (Glienicker Bridge) which links Berlin and Potsdam. In Prussian Arcadia new buildings contrast markedly with the old cultural landscape, the scene has lost some of its beauty. At the **jetty in Potsdam** the traffic roars by and seems unbelievably loud.

A griffin watches over the entrance to Klein-Glienicke park

the 19th century by Peter Joseph Lenné. A menagerie, established in 1822 with exotic animals, became the basis for the Zoologischer Garten (Zoological Garden) (➤ 126). About 60 peacocks live on the quiet island today.

8–9

The Havel widens into the **Sacrower See** (Lake Sacrow), which lies on the other side of the former border between East and West. Where the houses come to an end was where the "death strip" ran behind the greenery. The **Heilandskirche** (Church of the Saviour) on the bank of the Sacrower See, formerly part of the castle and park landscape, remained inaccessible until the fall of the Wall. Ludwig Persius designed the basilica (1841–4), which is regarded as a prototype for the Friedenskirche (Church of Peace) in Park Sanssouci (➤ 170).

9–10

The **Volkspark Klein-Glienicke** (People's Park) slips by on the left. You can see the columns of Schinkel's casino, and his Grosse Neugierde (Great Curiosity), a teahouse with a view, before sweeping under the

Artificial ruins were fashionable when the small castle on the Pfaueninsel (Peacock Island) was built

nephew of Friedrich II. Here he secretly met Wilhelmine Enke, on whom he later, as Friedrich Wilhelm III, bestowed the title of Countess of Lichtenau. She bore him five children and he died in her arms in 1797. She is said to have designed and furnished the small castle in the style of artificial ruins popular at the time. The landscaped park on the island was designed at the beginning of

KÖPENICK

Walk

2

A robbery and a "daring escapade" made Köpenick famous 100 years ago. And it is attractive as well, as stretches of water, chains of hills, woods and heath landscape are all a feature of Berlin's most southeasterly district.

DISTANCE: 2km (1¼ miles) **TIME:** 1.5 hours
START POINT: Köpenick Town Hall [tram] Köpenick, tram No 63
END POINT: River baths on Gartenstrasse

A walk through the old town seems like a trip in the country.

1–2

Köpenick gained notoriety in 1906, when, with the aid of a few soldiers, a shoemaker dressed in uniform arrested the major and "dispatched" him together with his wife to Berlin. He then seized the city treasury and disappeared himself in the direction of the capital. The escapade is recorded in the personal files at the police headquarters and is told in Carl Zuckmayer's well-known play, the *Captain of Köpenick*, performed for the first time in 1931. Today when it appears on the programme of the Maxim Gorki Theatre, Berliners jostle for a seat. The **Backsteinrathaus** (brick town hall) was at that time one

year old and is still standing today. A permanent exhibition documents the daring escapade. A bronze of the trickster stands in front of the town hall.

2–3

Köpenick's idyllic old town island suffers due to the traffic which buffets it. Henriette Lustig, the washerwoman to whom a monument with washboard was erected in the green area in front of the castle, on the Frauentog, lived at **Alter Markt 4**. In **Katzengraben** there are renovated colonial houses: No 6 dates back to 1683 and No 11 had already been rebuilt as early as 1869. In Freiheit street, the Elector had the ground raised and houses for 70 Huguenots built at the end of the 17th century. The street was named **Freiheit** (Freedom) because the houses were not subject to tax. When in the GDR era the bus drove from the new district into the old town, the stop was called out as usual, and on some occasions the driver called

Seat of the mayors of Köpenick

"Freedom for all" – short pause –
"who want to get off". A little
daring, and not everyone smiled...

3–4

Opposite the Alt-Köpenick road is
the access to the **Schlossinsel**
(Castle Island). Earlier, Slavic
ramparts stood here and in the
12th century a castle. Today a
wooden bridge leads through the
baroque portal. The baroque
castle was commissioned by
Elector Friedrich Wilhelm for
his son Friedrich III. But after
his father's death he moved
to Berlin and the castle remained unfinished. What you
see today is only the right
wing of the planned building.
Following its renovation it is
scheduled to house an arts and
crafts museum.

4–5

Past the Frauentog, a bay on the
Dahme, the route leads to the **Kietz**,
a fishing settlement mentioned as
early as 1209, with rough cobbles

Taking a Break

At the **Flussbadeanstalt** (river baths) you can relax
with a drink and just enjoy the view of
Schlossinsel (Castle Island).

and small houses whose doors and eaves are
decorated, in some cases with guild emblems.
There are no fishermen here today. The
houses have been attractively renovated by
architects. Something unique can be found
behind the door of Gartenstrasse 5: river baths
(Flussbadeanstalt), which have been here
since 1877. Those who wish can cool off by
jumping in the Dahme.

Berlin's last remaining river baths

KÖPENICK

Spree

KATZENGRABEN

LÜDERSSTR.

ALTER
MARKT

FREIHEIT ③

SCHUSSLER-
PLATZ

KIRCHSTR.

ROSENSTR.

JÄGERSTR.

KIETZER STR.

② KÖPENICKER STR.

BÖTTCHER
STR.

LINDENSTR.

ALTSTADT

★

① Town hall

MÜGGELHEIMER STR.

ANTONSTR.

MÜGGELHEIMER STR.

Kietz

KAUMANNSTR.

KIETZER
GASSE

BREITE
GASSE

GARTEN-
STR.

KIETZ

JUDISG.

AUISENSTR.

GARTENSTR.

Frauentog

④ Schloss-
insel

River baths ⑤

Dahme

LANGE BRÜCKE

0 ___ 200 metres
0 ___ 200 yards

3 THE WALL
Cycle Tour

It extended 160km (99 miles) around West Berlin, but even Berliners often don't recall where it was. A dozen years after the demolition of the bulwark that separated the world into East and West the border strip is still recognisable in

DISTANCE: 7km (4 miles) (Bike hire ► 36) **TIME:** 1.5 hours
START POINT: Potsdamer Platz ✚ 192 A1 🚇 Potsdamer Platz
END POINT: Oberbaumbrücke ✚ 198 C3 🚇 Warschauer Strasse

parts: in the city centre parts of the 43.1km (27 miles) of inner city Wall exist as cobbled stripes in bitumen, on the outskirts of the city the Wall can be seen as a break in the green. This tour is the beginning of the designated Wall cycle route.

1–2

The route begins at **Potsdamer Platz** (▶ 93). At **Leipziger Platz**, directly beside it, two segments of Wall have been preserved. On the corner of Stresemann and Köthener Strasse, a double row of cobblestones marks the Wall's path. The cycle route follows the west side of **Stresemannstrasse,** which lay in the border zone. The Hinterland Wall was on the eastern side of the street. Three

Starting point for the Wall cycle route

Potsdamer Platz was the most traffic-intensive intersection in the city up until World War II. In 1943 bombs destroyed the square and its surroundings. Weinhaus Huth, built in 1912 with a modern steel frame, withstood the tremors whereas the traditionally constructed buildings collapsed. It was later earmarked for demolition to make way for a city highway, but this was never built. "Schwarzmarkt" ("black market") was the name given to a flea market which took place here in the period following the fall of the Wall. Today Potsdamer Platz is the new centre of reunified Berlin. On the former site of Potsdamer Bahnhof (railway station), from which Prussia's first rail route (to Potsdam) began in 1838, a service industry complex, alongside Tilla-Durieux-Park, has been developed.

of its original elements, which the Berlin Senate presented to Kofi Annan, General Secretary of the United Nations, as a gift have been erected in front of the UN building in New York. Fifteen other painted segments of the Wall and a watchtower on Stresemann Strasse are classified as historical monuments.

2–3

The Wall continued to Niederkirchnerstrasse, directly past the **Martin-Gropius-Bau** (Martin Gropius building) (▶108). Directly opposite on the other side of the Wall, in the **Preussischer Landtag** (Prussian parliament building), the seat of Prussian parliament from 1899 to 1934, the first GDF government sat. Later the Staatssicherheit or "Stasi"

(National Security) installed bugging devices on the roof for intercepting radio communication in West Berlin. On 29 April, 1993, the first plenary session of the House of Representatives of Berlin took place here.

3–4

A copper strip marks the Wall route. **Topographie des Terrors** (Topography of Terror) is the name given to the former Prince Albrecht grounds, the headquarters of the SS (National Security), Gestapo (Secret Police) during the Nazi era. A portion of the Wall is preserved here. At the intersection of Wilhelmstrasse and Zimmerstrasse, a sign indicates Nazi Germany's Air Force Ministry (1935–6), in which the GDR was founded in

1949. Today the building houses the **Bundesfinanzministerium** (Federal Ministry of Finance). The wall frieze of marching workers (1952) is fired in Meissen porcelain. Directly opposite, Wolfgang Rüppel erected an answer to this in 2001 with a 24m (26-yard) long mural, sunken into the ground, as a memorial to the people's revolt of 17 June, 1953.

4–5

In Zimmerstrasse the border route is cobbled. **Checkpoint Charlie** (▶ 56) was at the corner of Friedrichstrasse. In front of house No 26 in Zimmerstrasse a memorial is dedicated to Peter Fechter, shot in August 1962 as he tried to escape to the West. A colourful new building (1994–6) was designed by Aldo Rossi for Charlotten-and

Taking a Break

In **Café Adler** opposite the Wall museum, refreshments are available, with a view of Checkpoint Charlie.

Markgrafenstrasse. On the corner of Jerusalemer and Zimmerstrasse, border soldier Reinhold Huhn was shot in June 1962 as he

tried to stop people escaping through a tunnel. The GDR named Schützenstrasse (Marksman Street) after the "socialist hero".

5–6

Axel Springer's **Verlagshaus** (publishing house) was built next to the Wall in 1966, as a sign of his belief in reunification. Axel-Springer-Strasse was named in 1995, on the 10th anniversary of his death. The Wall cobblestones turn into Kommandantenstrasse and continue behind the school at the end of Alexandrinenstrasse. The residents of Sebastianstrasse looked out upon nothing but wall for 28 years. At the intersection with Prinzenstrasse lay the **Heinrich-Heine-Strasse border crossing** for German citizens. An art installation in the U-Bahn tunnel is a memorial to this.

6–7

Follow the line of cobblestones to the intersection of Waldemar and Luckauer Strasse. Our route continues over the Luisenstädtischer Kanal, turns left into Leuschnerdamm and past the children's

The colourful East Side Gallery

Yesterday a warning, today a reminder of the border

farm to Engelbecken. The Wall ran along Bethaniendamm behind the **Künstlerhaus Bethanien** (▶ 147). Cross Köpenicker Strasse and **Schillingbrücke** to Friedrichshain, where the border lay on the western bank, but the Wall on the eastern bank of the Spree. On Mühlenstrasse pass Ostbahnhof and continue past **East Side Gallery** (▶ 139) and the former **Oberbaumbrücke crossing for West Berliners.**

GETTING ADVANCE INFORMATION

Websites
- www.berlin.de
- www.btm.de

In Germany
Berlin Tourismus
Marketing GmbH
Am Karlsbad 11
10785 Berlin
☎ (030) 25 00 25

In the UK
German National Tourist
Office
PO Box 2695
London W1A 3TN
☎ 020 7317 0908

BEFORE YOU GO

WHAT YOU NEED

- ● Required
- ○ Suggested
- ▲ Not required

	UK	USA	Canada	Australia	Ireland	France	Netherlands	Spain
Passport/National Identity Card	●	●	●	●	●	●	●	●
Visa	▲	▲	▲	▲	▲	▲	▲	▲
Onward or Return Ticket	▲	▲	▲	▲	▲	▲	▲	▲
Health Inoculations (tetanus and polio)	▲	▲	▲	▲	▲	▲	▲	▲
Health Documentation (▶ 188, Health)	●	●	●	●	●	●	●	●
Travel Insurance (▶ 188)	○	○	○	○	○	○	○	○
Driving Licence (national)	●	●	●	●	●	●	●	●
Third party Car Insurance Certificate	●	n/a	n/a	n/a	●	●	●	●
Car Registration Document	●	n/a	n/a	n/a	●	●	●	●

WHEN TO GO

Berlin

High season   Low season

JAN	FEB	MAR	APR	MAY	JUN	JUL	AUG	SEP	OCT	NOV	DEC
2°C	3°C	8°C	13°C	19°C	22°C	24°C	23°C	19°C	13°C	7°C	3°C

Sun   Cloudy   Wet   Sun/ Showers

The temperatures indicated are the average **daytime temperatures** in the
respective months. The **most pleasant time to visit** Berlin is from May to September. Berlin is a summer city; it offers a wealth of outdoor events and takes on the
flair of cities located in more southerly latitudes. But the city also has plenty to
attract visitors in autumn and winter who come to experience its culture. The dry
cold, which can sometimes be cutting and penetrate right into the bones, can be
avoided in museums and restaurants. For this reason Berlin enjoys an increasing
number of visitors particularly around Christmas and New Year. Easter is also a
popular time for visits to Berlin.

GETTING THERE

Berlin is serviced by air from 167 cities in 53 countries. Passengers from the USA, domestic locations and western Europe land at **Tegel** (TXL), some domestic flights land in **Tempelhof** (THF), and flights from eastern Europe, Asia and most charter flights land in **Schönefeld** (SXF).

Domestic flights in Germany are relatively expensive, whereas various airlines regularly offer cheaper flights from elsewhere in Europe. Check with airlines, travel agents or on the internet for current best deals.

By Train Berlin can be reached from all directions by IC, ICE, EuroCity and InterRegio trains. The central station in the western city centre is **Bahnhof Zoologischer Garten**, located at Hardenbergplatz 11 in Charlottenberg. The inner city in the east can be reached via **Ostbahnhof**, at Strasse der Pariser Kommune 5 in Friedrichshain. Some trains from the east terminate at **Bahnhof Lichtenberg**, located at Weitlingstrasse 22. Train services to and from Hamburg arrive at and depart from **Bahnhof Spandau**, on Seegefelder Strasse. The **motorail train** is loaded at Bahnhof Wannsee, at Kronprinzessinenweg in Zehlendorf.

By Car Autobahns (motorways) run from Hamburg and Rostock (A24), Hannover (A2), München (Munich) via Leipzig (A9), from Dresden (A13), Frankfurt/Oder (A12) and Stettin (A11) to Berlin. Exits on the Berliner Ring lead to the various districts.

TIME

Berlin is in the Central European time zone, i.e. one hour ahead of Greenwich Mean Time. In March clocks are adjusted one hour forwards for summer time (GMT +1), until October.

CURRENCY AND FOREIGN EXCHANGE

Currency Germany is one of the European countries to use a single currency, the **Euro** (€). The official abbreviation for the Euro is EUR. Euro notes are available in the following denominations: €5, €10, €20, €50, €100, €200 and €500; coins to the value of 1, 2 and 5 euro cents (bronze-coloured), 10, 20 and 50 euro cents (gold-coloured), and the €1 and €2 coins are available.
An exchange rate calculator is available on the internet: www.oanda.com.

Exchange Exchange bureaux can be found close to main railway stations and airports. **Travellers' cheques** can be cashed at all banks, whose branches are plentiful throughout the city. All transactions are subject to a commission charge. Outside of bank opening hours, **ATMs** (Geldautomat) are available in many locations.

Credit cards are accepted in almost all hotels, restaurants and shops. VISA and MasterCard cards with four-digit PINs can be used at most ATMs.

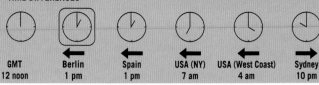

TIME DIFFERENCES

GMT	Berlin	Spain	USA (NY)	USA (West Coast)	Sydney
12 noon	← 1 pm	← 1 pm	← 7 am	← 4 am	→ 10 pm

WHEN YOU ARE THERE

CLOTHING SIZES

UK	Germany	USA	
36	46	36	
38	48	38	
40	50	40	
42	52	42	Suits
44	54	44	
46	56	46	
7	41	8	
7.5	42	8.5	
8.5	43	9.5	
9.5	44	10.5	Shoes
10.5	45	11.5	
11	46	12	
14.5	37	14.5	
15	38	15	
15.5	39/40	15.5	
16	41	16	Shirts
16.5	42	16.5	
17	43	17	
8	36	6	
10	38	8	
12	40	10	
14	42	12	Clothes
16	44	14	
18	46	16	
4.5	36	6	
5	37	6.5	
5.5	38	7	
6	39	7.5	Shoes
6.5	40	8	
7	41	8.51	

NATIONAL HOLIDAYS

1 Jan	New Year's Day
6 Jan	Three Kings Day
Mar/Apr	Good Friday, Easter Sunday and Monday
1 May	Labour Day
May/June	Ascension Day
May/June	Whit Sunday and Monday
3 Oct	Reunification Day
1 Nov	All Saints' Day
24 Dec	Christmas Eve
25, 26 Dec	Christmas
31 Dec	New Year's Eve

OPENING HOURS

○ Shops   ● Post Offices
● Offices   ● Museums/Monuments
● Banks   ● Pharmacies (Apotheke)

8 am 9 am 10 am noon 1 pm 2 pm 4 pm 5 pm 6 pm

☐ Morning   ▨ Midday   ☐ Evening

Shops Most shops are open Monday to Friday 10–8 and on Saturday 9–4. Shops which stock tourist supplies may also open on Sundays.

Banks Banks and savings banks (Sparkasse) are generally open from Monday to Friday 9 am until 2 or 3 pm, and until 6 pm on one day of the week. Some also open on Saturday mornings.

Museums Almost all Berlin museums are open from Tuesday to Sunday from 10 am until 6 pm. Some museums also open until 8 pm on Thursday. Museums which are open on Monday close on Tuesday instead.

EMERGENCY	110
POLICE	110
FIRE (and ambulance)	112
POISONING	(030) 192 40

PERSONAL SAFETY

Berlin is a relatively safe city for tourists. Small-scale criminal activity is limited to very busy areas such as Breidscheidplatz or bus route No 100, which are also frequented by pickpockets.

- Drivers needn't be alarmed by young people standing at the traffic lights at, most commonly, Grosser Stern or intersections in Kreuzberg. They offer to wash windscreens for 1 euro.
- Avoid almost empty S-Bahn trains heading east late at night.
- Parking lots such as Hasenheide should be avoided at night as drug dealers may be active there.
- Keep valuables in your hotel safe.

Police assistance:
 110 from any phone

TELEPHONES

There are two types of public telephone in Berlin: old-style yellow closed booths, and newer grey and pink open booths. Almost all require a *Telefonkarte* (telephone card) available at post offices, stationery shops and newsagents.

For overseas calls, after dialling the country code, the "0" is omitted from the area code, followed by the number.

International Dialing Codes
Dial 00 followed by

UK:	44
Ireland:	353
USA/Canada	1
Australia	61
Spain	34

POST

There are post offices in every district. Poste restante mail can only be collected from here. Post office branches have been set up in many stationery shops, where stamps may be bought, letters, small packages and parcels can be sent and money withdrawn. The post office at Neues Kanzlereck, on the corner of Kurfürstendamm and Joachimstaler Strasse, is open until 10 pm, and on Sundays and public holidays.

ELECTRICITY

The power supply in Germany is 220 volts. Sockets accept two-round-pin plugs. Travellers from outside continental Europe should use an adaptor.

TIPS/GRATUITIES

Generally restaurant, drinks and taxi bills are rounded up generously. 5 per cent is a good general rule.

Hotel porters	€1–2
Chambermaids	€1–2
Tour guides	on own discretion
Lavatory attendants	30 cents

EMBASSIES AND CONSULATES

UK	USA	Australia	Canada	Spain
☎ (030) 20 18 40	☎ (030) 238 51 74	☎ (030) 880 08 80	☎ (030) 20 31 20	☎ (030) 254 00

HEALTH

Insurance: Special travel health insurance is recommended, particularly for visitors from non-EU countries. Nationals of EU countries can obtain medical treatment at reduced cost with the relevant documentation (form E111 for Britons). Doctors are listed in the yellow pages of the telephone directory. The medical emergency service (Ärztlicher Bereitschaftsdienst) can be reached on (030) 31 00 31.

Dental Services: Dental treatment for non-German rvisitors can be expensive. The patient is given a bill, which he or she must claim on his or her health insurance in the patient's home country. The dental emergency service (Zahnärztliche Bereitsschaftsdient) can be reached on (030) 89 00 43 33.

Weather: In the middle of summer it can be hot in Berlin. Take care to protect yourself against sunburn and drink plenty of fluids.

Drugs: There are many pharmacies (Apotheke) selling prescription and non-prescription medicines. Medicines on foreign prescription can be obtained at the pharmacy at Joachimstaler Strasse 10 in Charlottenburg (tel: (030) 88 55 00 33).

Safe Water: Tap water is suitable for drinking, but the water from green pumps scattered throughout Berlin should not be consumed.

CONCESSIONS

Concessions are usually only granted to German residents who are unemployed, welfare recipients, soldiers, trainees or who have severe disabilities, on presentation of the appropriate ID. Children and groups of school students often receive concessions. Children pay reduced fares on public transport.

A day ticket is available for the **Museen des Preussischen Kulturbesitzes** (Museums of Prussian Cultural Heritage), costing 6 euros for a total of 17 museums. The **3-Tage-Museumspass** (3-day Museum Pass) for *SchauLust* museums in Berlin allows reduced entry to more than 50 museums (► 37).

TRAVELLING WITH A DISABILITY

Lifts and ramps for easy access to platforms are installed at 51 U-Bahn stations and 118 S-Bahn stations. Stations with facilities for visitors with disabilities are marked on the BVG (Berlin transport) network maps and city maps. Buses with ramps in the middle door that can be lowered to the ground are in use on more than 100 routes. Low-floored trams with ramps that can be lowered to the ground are in use on 14 routes. Vehicles with facilities for visitors with disabilities are identified on bus and tram timetables.

CHILDREN

Children are welcome in almost all hotels and restaurants. Children's theatre, cinemas, farms and programmes in museums are part of everyday life in Berlin.

LAVATORIES

Public lavatories can often be found near major sights. In many districts there are still some of the old urinals in dark green pavilions.

LOST PROPERTY

Zentrales Fundbüro (Central Lost Property Office): Platz der Luftbrücke 6, tel: (030) 75 60 31 01.

BERLIN PLACE NAMES

This guide uses the revised spelling "ss" for words like *Strasse* (street) and *Imbiss* (snack-bar), but you will often see the older spelling *Straße*, *Imbiß*. So remember: *ß* is equivalent to "ss".
The following German terms have been used throughout:
U-Bahn underground railway (subway)
S-Bahn overground (often overhead) local and regional railway
Reichstag the Federal German Parliament (➤ 52)

SURVIVAL PHRASES

Yes/no **Ja/nein**
Good morning **Guten Morgen**
Good afternoon **Guten Tag**
Good evening **Guten Abend**
Goodbye **Auf Wiedersehen**
How are you? **Wie geht es Ihnen?**
You're welcome **Bitte schön**
Please **Bitte**
Thank you **Danke**
Excuse me **Entschuldigung**
I'm sorry **Es tut mir Leid**
Do you have ...? **Haben Sie...?**
I'd like ... **Ich möchte ...**
How much is that? **Was kostet das?**
I don't understand **Ich verstehe nicht**
Do you speak English? **Spechen Sie Englisch?**
Open **Geöffnet** Closed **Geschlossen**
Push/pull **Drücken/Ziehen**
Women's lavatory **Damen**
Men's lavatory **Herren**

DAYS OF THE WEEK

Monday **Montag**
Tuesday **Tuesday**
Wednesday **Mittwoch**
Thursday **Donnerstag**
Friday **Freitag**
Saturday **Samstag**
Sunday **Sontag**

OTHER USEFUL WORDS & PHRASES

Yesterday **Gestern**
Today **Heute**
Tomorrow **Morgen**
Could you call a doctor please? **Könnten Sie bitte einen Arzt rufen?**
Do you have a vacant room? **Haben Sie ein Zimmer frei?**
- with bath/shower **mit Bad/Dusche**
Single room **Das Einzelzimmer**
Double room **Das Doppelzimmer**
One/two nights **Eins/Zwei Nächte**
How much per night? **Was kostet es pro Nacht?**

DIRECTIONS & GETTING AROUND

Where is...? **Wo ist...?**
- the train/bus station **die Bahnhof/Busbahnhof**
- the bank **die Bank**
– the nearest toilets **die nächsten Toiletten**
Turn left/right **Biegen Sie links ab/rechts ab**
Go straight on **Gehen Sie geradeaus**
Here/there **Hier/daar**
North **Norden**
East **Ost**
South **Süden**
West **West**

NUMBERS

1	eins	13	dreizehn	30	dreissig	102	eins hundert zwei
2	zwei	14	vierzehn	31	een en dertig	200	zwei hundert
3	drei	15	fünfzehn	32	twee en dertig	300	drei hundert
4	vier	16	sechzehn	40	vierzig	400	vier hundert
5	fünf	17	siebzehn	50	fünfzig	500	fünf hundert
6	sechs	18	achtzehn	60	sechzig	600	sechs hundert
7	sieben	19	neunzehn	70	siebzig	700	sieben hundret
8	acht	20	zwanzig	80	achtzig	800	acht hundret
9	neun	21	ein undzwanzig	90	neunzig	900	neun hundret
10	zehn			100	hundert	1,000	tausend
11	elf	22	twee en twintig	101	eins hundert eins		
12	zwölf						

A table for ..., please **Einen Tisch für ... bitte**

We have/haven't booked **Wir haben/haben nicht reserviert**

I'd like to reserve a table for ... people at ... **Ich möchte einen Tisch für ... Personen um ... reservieren**

I am a vegetarian **Ich bin Vegetarier**

May I see the menu, please? **Die Speisekarte bitter?**

Is there a dish of the day, please? **Gibt es ein Tagesgerich?**

We'd like something to drink **Wir möchten etwas zu trinken**

Do you have a wine list in English? **Haben Sie eine Weinkarte auf Englisch?**

This is not what I ordered **Das habe ich nicht bestellt**

Could we sit there? **Können wir dort sitzen?**

When do you open/close? **Wann machen Sie auf/zu?**

The food is cold **Das Essen ist kalt**

The food was excellent **Essen war ausgezeichnet**

Can I have the bill, please? **Wir möchten zahlen, bitte**

Is service included? **Ist das mit Bedienung?**

Breakfast **Das Frühstück**
Lunch **Das Mittagessen**
Dinner **Das Abendessen**

Starters **Die Vorspeise**
Main course **Das Hauptgericht**
Desserts **Die Nachspeisen**

Fish dishes **Fischgerichte**
Meat dishes **Fleischgerichte**
Fruit **Obst**
Vegetables **Gemüse**
Dish of the day **Das Tagesgericht**
Wine list **Die Weinkarte**

Salt **Das Salz**
Pepper **Der Pfeffer**

Knife **Das Messer**
Fork **Die Gabel**
Spoon **Der Löffel**

Waiter **Kellner**
Waitress **Kellnerin**

MENU A–Z

Äpfel Apples
Apfelsaft Apple juice
Apfelsinen Oranges
Aufschnitt Sliced cold meat
Austern Oysters
Belegte Brote Sandwiches
Birnen Pears
Blumenkohl Cauliflower
Brathähnchen Roast chicken
Bratwurst Fried sausage
Brokkoli Broccoli
Brötchen Bread roll
Creme Cream
Eintopf Casserole
Eisbein Knuckle of pork
Ente Duck
Erbsen Peas
Erdbeeren Strawberries
Fasan Pheasant
Fenchel Fennel
Flunder Flounder
Forelle Trout
Frühstücksspeck Grilled bacon
Gans Goose
Gekochtes Ei Boiled egg
Gulasch Goulash
Grüne Bohnen Green beans
Heilbutt Halibut
Hering Herring
Himbeeren Raspberries
Honig Honey
Hummer Lobster
Kabeljau Cod
Kaffee Coffee
Kalbsleber Calf's liver
Karotten Carrots
Kartoffeln Potatoes
Käse Cheese
Käsekuchen Cheesecake

Kasseler Smoked pork loin
Kirschen Cherries
Krabben Shrimps
Kohl Cabbage
Konfitüre Preserves
Kopfsalat Lettuce
Lachs Salmon
Lammbraten Roast lamb
Lauch Leeks
Mais Sweet corn
Milch Milk
Obsttorte Fruit tart
Obstsalat Fruit salad
Orangensaft Orange juice
Paprika Pepper
Pfirsiche Peaches
Pflaumen Plums
Pilze Mushrooms
Rinderbraten Roast beef
Rotkohl Red cabbage
Rührei Scrambled egg
Schinken Ham
Scholle Plaice
Schokoladentorte Chocolate cake
Schweinebraten Roast pork
Schweinekotelett Pork chop
Seezunge Sole
Spargel Asparagus
Spiegelei Fried egg
Spinat Spinach
Suppen Soups
Tee Tea
Tomaten Tomatoes
Vanillepudding Custard
Wiener Schnitzel Veal escalope
Weintrauben Grapes
Wild Venison
Zucchini Courgettes
Zwiebeln Onions

Streetplan

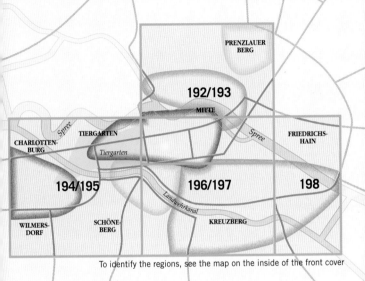

PRENZLAUER
BERG

192/193

MITTE

Spree

TIERGARTEN

Spree

FRIEDRICHS-
HAIN

CHARLOTTEN-
BURG

Tiergarten

194/195

196/197

198

Landwehrkanal

WILMERS-
DORF

SCHÖNE-
BERG

KREUZBERG

To identify the regions, see the map on the inside of the front cover

Legend

——————	Main road		Park
————	Other road		Important building
- - - - -	Tunnel		Featured place of interest
═══════	Pedestrianised way	◎	U-Bahn station
——————	Rail line	◉	S-Bahn (local rail) station
————	U-Bahn (underground) line		

0	250	500	750	1000 metres
0	250	500	750	1000 yards

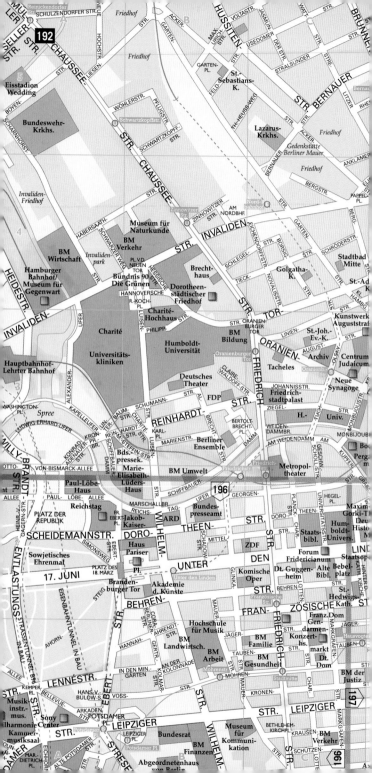

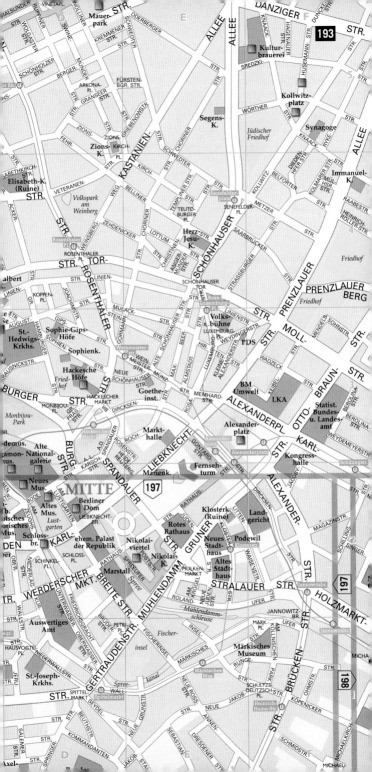

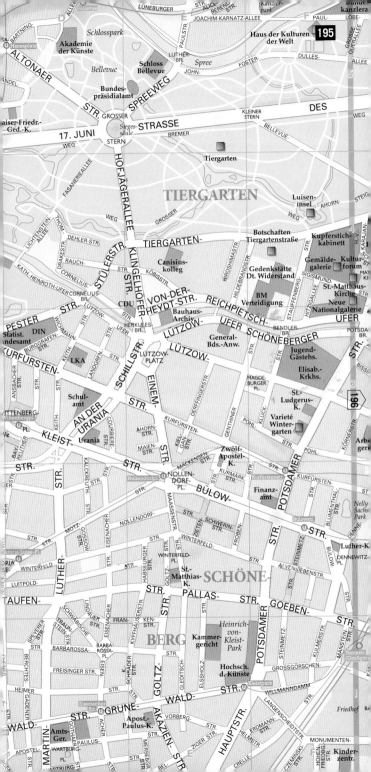

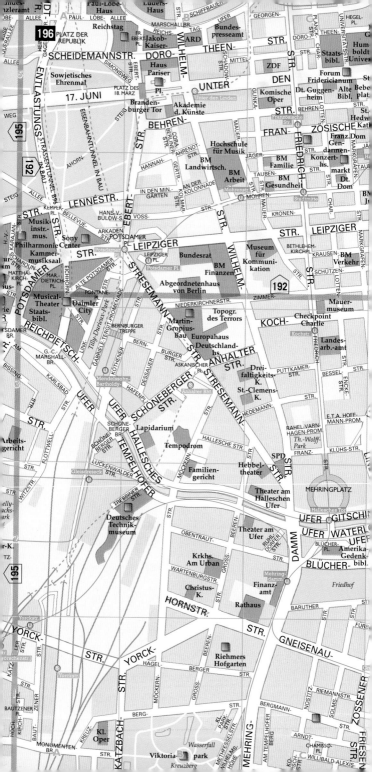

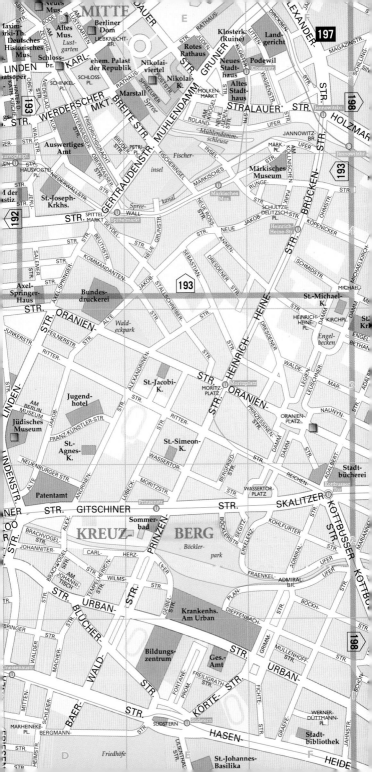

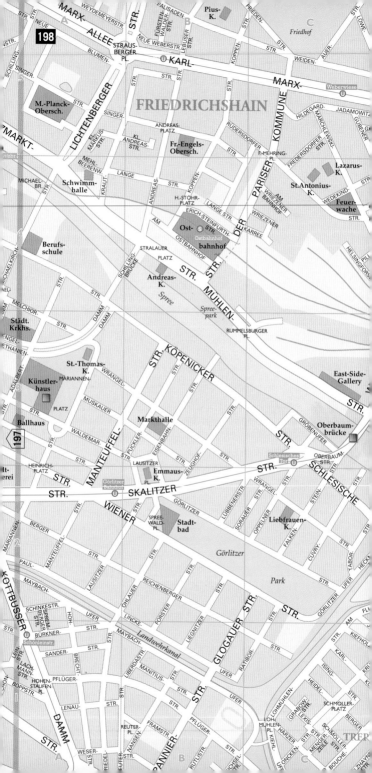

Index

Picture credits

SPIRAL GUIDES

Questionnaire

Dear Traveler

Your comments, opinions and recommendations are very important to us. So please help us to improve our travel guides by taking a few minutes to complete this simple questionnaire.

Send to: Spiral Guides, MailStop 66, 1000 AAA Drive, Heathrow, FL 32746–5063

Your recommendations...

We always encourage readers' recommendations for restaurants, nightlife or shopping – if your recommendation is added to the next edition of the guide, we will send you a FREE AAA Spiral Guide of your choice. Please state below the establishment name, location and your reasons for recommending it.

_____

_____

_____

_____

_____

Please send me AAA Spiral_____

(see list of titles inside the back cover)

About this guide...

Which title did you buy?

_____ **AAA Spiral**

Where did you buy it? _____

When? m m / y y

Why did you choose a AAA Spiral Guide? _____

_____

_____

_____

Did this guide meet your expectations?

Exceeded ☐   Met all ☐   Met most ☐   Fell below ☐

Please give your reasons _____

_____

_____

_____

continued on next page...

Were there any aspects of this guide that you particularly liked?

Is there anything we could have done better?

About you...

Name (Mr/Mrs/Ms) ______

Address ______

______ Zip ______

Daytime tel nos. ______

Which age group are you in?

Under 25 ☐ 25–34 ☐ 35–44 ☐ 45–54 ☐ 55–64 ☐ 65+ ☐

How many trips do you make a year?

Less than one ☐ One ☐ Two ☐ Three or more ☐

Are you a AAA member? Yes ☐ No ☐

Name of AAA club ______

About your trip...

When did you book? m m/ y y When did you travel? m m/ y y

How long did you stay? ______

Was it for business or leisure? ______

Did you buy any other travel guides for your trip? ☐ Yes ☐ No

If yes, which ones? ______

Thank you for taking the time to complete this questionnaire.

All information is for AAA internal use only and will NOT be distributed outside the organization to any third parties.